POLICY ANALYSIS FOR PRACTICE

Applying social policy

Paul Spicker

First published in Great Britain in June 2006 by

The Policy Press
University of Bristol
Fourth Floor
Beacon House
Queen's Road
Bristol BS8 1QU
UK

Tel +44 (0)117 331 4054
Fax +44 (0)117 331 4093
e-mail tpp-info@bristol.ac.uk
www.policypress.org.uk

© Paul Spicker 2006

British Library Cataloguing in Publication Data
A catalogue record for this book is available from the British Library.

Library of Congress Cataloging-in-Publication Data
A catalog record for this book has been requested.

ISBN-10 1 86134 825 8 paperback
ISBN-13 978 1 86134 825 8 paperback
ISBN-10 1 86134 826 6 hardcover
ISBN-13 978 1 86134 826 5 hardcover

Cover design by Qube Design Associates, Bristol.
Printed and bound in Great Britain by Hobbs the Printers Ltd, Southampton.

Contents

Preface

This book is intended to introduce students and practitioners to the concepts, methods and skills required for policy analysis in practice. 'Policy analysis' can understood in two main senses. Policy analysis in the UK usually refers to the analysis *of* policy – understanding the structures and processes which relate to policy making. Policy analysis in the US is more usually treated as analysis *for* policy – helping to make decisions about what course to follow, and reviewing what effects different measures might have. That, by contrast with the first approach, is the main sense in which 'policy analysis' is used in this book. Readers who are familiar with some of the standard approaches in the UK, like books by Parsons or Hudson and Lowe,[1] may be surprised how little direct relationship there is between their concerns and the agenda of this book. This is not a criticism of the value of understanding structures and processes, but this book is trying to do something quite different. There is a particular shortage of this kind of material in the UK, but practitioners here need to understand analysis for policy as much as their American counterparts do.

The book mixes approaches from two overlapping fields of study. The first is Public Administration. Most British books on Public Administration are concerned with the process by which policy is made and implemented. The structure of the book is based on the 'rational-comprehensive' model of planning, which reviews:

- the environment in which policy takes place;
- the aims of policy;
- the selection of methods;
- the process of implementation; and
- evaluation.

Obviously, it is important to have some understanding of structures and processes in order to be able to work effectively in practice, but this is not the main focus. Rather, it is on the skills and methods which can be used to deal with problems in practice.

The second field of study is Social Policy. By contrast with Public Administration, Social Policy is focused less on process than on the substantive content of policies. The principal areas relate to policy and administrative practice in health administration, social security, education, employment services, community care and housing management; social problems, including criminology, disability, unemployment, mental health and old age; issues relating to social disadvantage, including 'race', gender and poverty; and the range of collective social responses to these conditions. The study of the subject is concerned with:

- the general application of social science disciplines to these issues, such as sociology, economics and political science;
- specific methods and approaches relevant to the areas of study of these subject areas, including policy analysis, social planning methods, the evaluation of organisational processes and service delivery, and the management of social services; and
- the development of skills for application in these contexts, including, for example, welfare rights, social research methods and social planning.

Social Policy was conceived as an applied subject. The field was developed to meet the needs of public and voluntary sector administrators who needed to know about the problems and processes they would be dealing with. In the course of the last 20 years or so, however, teaching of the subject in British universities has become progressively more divorced from its practical and vocational roots. Although the practical issues the subject used to be mainly focused on are not treated as central in the field of Social Policy nowadays, they have not gone away. On the contrary, they have developed very substantially, and there is a rich and varied literature about them. Issues like strategic planning, partnership working and user participation have become part of the language of everyday practice in central and local government. There is a new administrative language, covering topics like performance indicators, targets and audit. Beyond that, we have seen the growth of a range of relatively new concepts – issues like empowerment, voice and quasi-markets. There are a range of new techniques, obviously including changes in information and communication technology, but including focus groups, interactive approaches to consultation and participative research. At a time when most people working in Social Policy had lost interest in social administration, the field has been growing, developing and changing. This book is concerned with a particular aspect of the applied focus of Social Policy, which is its application to policy making and review. (This is only part of the agenda for an applied course in Social Policy – the other parts are professional skills and public sector management.) The areas which this book covers include many which are closely related to employment in social administration and public service.

The kinds of work that students in Social Policy are most likely to do call for the sort of skills and techniques discussed in this book.

Policy analysis for practice has developed from teaching on a Master's in Public Administration (MPA) at the Robert Gordon University. I owe thanks to Geraldine Wooley and Coryn Barclay for comments, and to my colleague Kirsteen Davidson, who co-wrote the case study on gender mainstreaming.

Paul Spicker,
May 2006

Notes on the author

Paul Spicker holds the Grampian Chair of Public Policy at the Robert Gordon University, Aberdeen, and is Director of the Centre for Public Policy and Management. His research includes studies of poverty, need, disadvantage and service delivery; he has worked as a consultant for a range of agencies in social welfare provision. His books include:

Stigma and social welfare (Croom Helm, 1984)

Principles of social welfare (Routledge, 1988)

Social housing and the social services (Longman, 1989)

Poverty and social security: concepts and principles (Routledge, 1993)

Social policy: themes and approaches (Prentice Hall, 1995)

Planning for the needs of people with dementia (with D S Gordon, Avebury, 1997)

Social protection: a bilingual glossary (co-edited with J-P Révauger, Mission-Recherche, 1998)

Social policy in a changing society (with Maurice Mullard, Routledge, 1998)

The international glossary on poverty (co-editor with David Gordon, Zed, 1999)

The welfare state: a general theory (Sage Publications, 2000).

ONE

The nature of policy analysis

Policy analysis

There are three main areas of applied policy work: policy formation, public sector management, and policy analysis and review.

- *Policy formation.* The formation and development of policy depends on knowledge of the specific subject area and ideas about options and approaches. Studies in this field focus on what policies are, what they do, and how else they might be done. Because this is often done in an attempt to bring about change in policy, or to defend particular approaches, it is sometimes referred to as 'policy advocacy'.[2]
- *Public sector management* is mainly concerned with the process of administering policy, implementation and managing organisations. The skills required include project management, resource management and working with people.
- *Policy analysis and review.* This is about examining policy – finding out and assessing what is happening; monitoring implementation; and evaluation, or finding out whether policies do what they are supposed to do.

Although there are references in this book to all these activities, *Policy analysis for practice* is mainly concerned with the third area, policy analysis and review. Policy analysis works by trying to establish the criteria by which policies can be judged, to find out how they operate, and to see whether they produce the effects they are supposed to produce. This book introduces the concepts, approaches and techniques which are used to examine policy in practice. It has a direct application to an expanding set of job opportunities, concerned with social administration, service planning and delivery, and strategic public service management.

The work of the policy analyst

There is no agreement about what a 'policy analyst' is or does. An advertisement in June 2002 for 'policy analysts' in the Scottish Executive generated widespread confusion in the press, with the suspicion that what the Executive was looking for were political advisors. Policy analysis is more pedestrian: the Executive was looking for people with the skills to say what kinds of approach might be possible and whether the policies worked or not. This is, broadly, what many civil servants, administrators and local government officers do. There are many people who work as policy analysts, but in the UK they are not often called that.

I started to write this book on a Wednesday morning, and the jobs advertised in the morning's newspaper included posts like these:

- *Operations Manager*, Housing Association offering housing and support for people with either a learning disability or a mental health problem. You will be able to demonstrate:
  - understanding of issues and the environment of community care, including relevant legislation;
  - knowledge of the role and function of housing associations;
  - experience of service funding negotiations;
  - experience of obtaining and managing new service developments;
  - knowledge of drafting and advising on policy.
- *Planning and Development Officers*, Children and Family Services. You will need to have a thorough understanding of current issues, and the ability to think strategically and critically. Both postholders will hold key positions in Departmental and inter-agency service development, and will be involved in the preparation of statutory plans in consultation with colleagues, service users and other organisations.
- *Research and Information Officer*, Social Work. The Research and Information section provides research, service evaluation and management information support to Departmental managers and planners; produces statutory and Departmental performance information and statistical returns to government; supports 'Best Value' service reviews, including consumer research; undertakes work on resource allocation, and develops population models of need and demand for planning purposes.

There are pages upon pages of these adverts. Many of them are looking for people with specific experience of a client group, particular knowledge of agency structures and managerial experience; but they are also looking for a range of skills. They want people who can negotiate with others involved in the field, develop plans and programmes, deliver reports, and work out whether or not policy is being effective. These are the skills of policy analysis. They are generally wanted in local government, voluntary sector organisations and specialist agencies. There are few areas of public service in which they are not at least relevant.

There are also people who work exclusively as policy analysts, even if they are not often called that. Consultancy and research work often requires a similar range of skills and methods, and some of the examples in this text are drawn from my own work in this field. For the purposes of this book, the kinds of problems which are being considered are the kinds of problems consultants are asked to deal with. Unlike managers or practitioners, who generally have to find room for work related to policy or strategy in competition with the rest of their work, consultants are left free to look at every aspect of a problem or issue. The classic model of the consultant is 'Star Trek': Captain Kirk beams down into an alien environment with no preparation or knowledge of the situation, and little more than his wits and principles of engagement to work by, and has to find a solution for everyone's problems before the end of the episode.

This is not so far from reality as it might appear at first. The advantage of starting here is that the situation lends itself to comprehensive analysis, and in particular it can reflect the position of the student who is analysing, commenting and reporting on policies from outside the agency. At the same time, it can be remote from the experience of people who undertake policy analysis within an organisation. People who are working in a particular setting do not start cold. They will have a series of relationships, good and bad, which will help or hinder the work they are trying to do. They have a status in the organisation, which conveys a sense of expectation: it can be difficult for people with junior status to mobilise support for projects from others who are senior to them. Some of the same considerations apply to external consultants – they are often taken to 'belong' to the person who hired them, or brought them in to the organisation. (It is also possible, of course, that agencies bring in outsiders because they do not have any particular commitment to the policy, and can drop it afterwards; but that is the kind of problem policy analysts have to cope with.) These kinds of issues can still be considered in the context of a comprehensive model.

Policy analysis and social science

Policy analysis is an exercise in applied social science. It begins with a set of issues or problems and tries to apply insights from different sources to the problems in hand. There are many different types of academic course which are based on a wide range of approaches from different social sciences: examples are general courses on social policy or public sector management, and specific professional courses for social workers, housing managers and health administrators. These courses usually draw on material from a range of social sciences. Economics and sociology are particularly important, although other material can be drawn from philosophy, psychology, history and law.

Academic studies provide both tools and techniques for the task, and specific knowledge. The knowledge base which is most relevant to this field is part of what used to be called 'social administration', although in most places the term has been replaced by the more general term of 'social policy'. Social administration is concerned specifically with the operation and delivery of social services. It is often castigated in the literature as being far too much concerned with description, and too little with analysis. If this was ever true, it had largely ceased to be true by the late 1960s, when academic discussions of the subject started to flourish. The literature of social administration covers issues like service organisation, delivery, management, needs and relationships with users. Many of the most interesting developments in social policy since 1990 have been issues in social administration: examples are community care, needs assessments, quasi-markets, care management and user empowerment. Many of the practical issues which matter in the field are issues in social administration; examples are corporate planning, service rationing, joint working and the analysis of institutional racism. This is a specialist literature, mainly now contained in social policy and professional courses preparing people to work in the social services. Social administration is related to public policy mainly because general issues and principles, some of which are covered in this book, apply across and between services. It is different from public policy because social administration is focused on content and results, rather than process. Social administration is strongly concerned with practical policies to improve welfare – meeting need, dealing with disadvantage and promoting social justice.

Sociology contributes a basic understanding of many concepts which are fundamental to policy, including social problems, inequality and social exclusion, and analyses of key topics, including, for example, health, education, the family, 'race' and gender. It provides some of the staple tools of policy analysis, including the construction of social indicators, identification of social processes, the use of social research methods and some of the literature on evaluation.

Economics is important for two reasons. The first is that economic approaches and information are a basic part of policy work. Concepts like marginal cost, cost-benefit analysis and efficiency are part of policy analysis, and analysts need to be familiar with them. Second, analysts have to know enough to deal with the economic arguments. I went once to an international social security conference on targeting and incentives to work, where a group of American economists were revealing the Truth to the lesser orders in the rest of the world. I discussed this with a delegate from a country in West Africa, where most people lived in poverty, nearly a fifth of all children died before they were five and whose social security system barely covered a tenth of the population. What, I asked him, has this stuff on incentives to work got to do with you? His answer was, I thought, a very good one. He explained that although the problems the Americans were discussing were quite irrelevant, he had to deal with international organisations, like the World Bank and the United Nations, which talked the same language. He had to get to grips with this sort of thing if he wanted to deal with them.

Among the other areas which might be useful, law deserves a special mention. Legal studies are often seen, and far too often taught to practitioners, as a long list of 'dos' and 'don'ts'. Even at that level, the law is potentially useful: human rights, data protection or negligence are commonly part of the background noise of policy decisions, but just occasionally there might be some reason to put them in the foreground. It is certainly true that, even if some legal principles change and develop, others (like natural justice, which I refer to later) are long established as part of the everyday meat of administrative decisions, and analysts ought to be familiar with them. But beyond this, there are also advantages to understanding legal reasoning. Many laws are devised, not to establish the limits of right and wrong, but to draw a line between those rules that might work in practice, and those that won't; it is a line of reasoning that policy makers may also need to follow.

Because policy analysis is practically oriented, many of the problems will be concerned with the specifics of the area where they are applied, and they will mainly be considered by practitioners. Some of the issues can only be addressed by practitioners, and the role of the policy analyst will be to clarify problems – to ask questions and organise material, so that the practitioners themselves can come to a view. It often happens, in this process, that the best answers an analyst can provide are answers which the practitioners knew anyway. (The time to invoice people for payment, one consultancy book suggests, is before the customers realise they could have done it themselves.) At the same time, some of the skills of social policy analysts will be alien to practitioners. Some areas of policy have been colonised by particular professions, but that does not mean that the skills of that profession are needed to do the job. Doctors learn how to take an appendix out on the kitchen table, which they are unlikely nowadays to do in practice, but relatively few know what the options are for organising an appointments system, even if that might be rather more relevant to the way they actually work. Social workers are responsible, in the UK, for community care, but most social workers' training is geared to understand needs and identifying individual responses, rather than the service planning and administration that go along with that.

Many of the administrative tasks undertaken by practitioners are treated as a matter of 'common sense'. Many agencies have a firmly held understanding of what 'common sense' means, and take a dim view of outsiders whose common sense is different. Many people who work within organisations, particularly at the lower levels, are expected to learn on the job. They learn from others who are working in the same setting, and they often come to hold similar views. Social services have their own 'ideologies' – interrelated sets of values, opinions and beliefs which relate to the practical issues of the work setting.[3] Often, these ideologies reflect common pressures and expectations from people outside. Police forces emphasise public order, not because public order offences are the most serious crimes, but because they will be subject to criticism if public order breaks down in a way that they will not be if crime rates increase generally. Social workers emphasise risk, because ultimately they are likely to be judged if things go wrong. Housing officers tend to emphasise equity, because there will be protests if some people are seen to be treated differently from others. These differences are reinforced by professional training, but they make sense in their own right: they reflect the demands of the job.

Skills for policy analysis

Anyone can set up shop as a policy analyst. Many of the people who work in the field have drifted into it, because they were in a job which required them to start doing it in practice. There may be no agreement about the job specification, but there is a task to perform, and the task calls for certain skills.

We can dispose of one myth immediately: analysts do not have to be able to do the job themselves to make relevant comments about a service. It is important for a policy analyst to gain some working knowledge of the area which is being investigated. There is a jargon to be learned; professionals in the field will want to communicate their concerns; users will need to be able to explain their experiences. The skills which are needed to do this, however, are not necessarily the skills of the relevant profession. It does not take a doctor to ask a patient about their treatment – in some circumstances, being associated with the medical profession may be an obstacle. It does not take a social worker to talk to the users of social work services. (Despite the impression one may gain from the specialist literature, these are not just 'service users'. They are *people*.) It is important, however, to be sensitive to the situation that people are in, and to know how to ask them the questions which will produce the answers. These are the basic skills of a researcher, and there are many fields in which people learn those skills.

Research

Much of the work which is involved in analysis is described in academic settings as 'research', although it is not necessarily research in the conventional sense: the main purpose is not to find things out, but to do what is necessary for practice. People who want to influence policy have to do many of the same things that researchers do. They need to understand the context in which the policy is being applied; they have to be able to identify the likely effects of policies, and to assess and evaluate the policy after it has been undertaken. This means that many of the skills and methods of researchers are important for policy analysts; they have to review sources of data, gather evidence and make judgments about the weight to give to different findings.

Newcomers to 'research' often assume that it involves particular approaches and techniques – like random samples, clipboards and boxes to tick. This is a mistake. There is no single way of doing things. Research can include any method of finding something out. This includes, among other methods:

- scholarship – finding things out by looking at books and archives;
- exploration – finding things out by searching, observation and enquiry;
- practice – finding things out through testing, experimenting, developing and implementing methods; and
- systematic investigation – finding things out by surveys, controlled experiments and other forms of scientific empirical examination.

There is no 'right' way to do research. Because methods can shape results unintentionally, however, the best approaches tend to be those which combine different approaches – in the jargon, 'triangulating' – in order to confirm issues from a range of perspectives.

The process of undertaking research can be broken down into four main tasks:

- selection and interpretation of the research problem;
- choosing methods;
- obtaining data; and
- processing and interpreting the data.

Selection and interpretation. In applied research, the selection of the research problem is often given; it is not usually open to a policy analyst, asked to look at the problems of poor families, to say 'let's look at the structure of capitalism instead'. There is still scope for interpretation – what, after all, is a poor family, and who should be excluded or included from the definition? This kind of selection is informed partly by theoretical considerations, but also by what it is feasible and practical for people to do.

Choosing methods. Research methods are almost infinitely flexible. Some things will be done as standard: a review of what other people have done and a collation of existing material. Beyond that, there is a very wide range of different research approaches and techniques, rooted in a range of academic disciplines. There is scope, then, for considerable imagination in what kinds of methods can be used and how they are applied. It tends to be true, of course, that imagination is not always appreciated; there is no research programme which cannot be subjected to methodological criticism, but programmes which follow well-worn paths are less vulnerable to scepticism than innovative ones.

Obtaining data. Research depends on getting hold of the people and sources from which information can be drawn. This is usually referred to in research primers as 'sampling', although the practical experience of many policy analysts is that the sample is often set before they appear, and something has to be done within those constraints which makes some kind of sense. The popular image of research tends to assume that it is 'representative'. Representative samples are drawn from a whole population, usually either on a random basis or by selection for a quota. Representative samples are intended to reflect the views of the whole population; this is useful in surveys of public opinion or consumer satisfaction. Ideally, a representative sample is taken by reproducing their characteristics – gender, age, ethnicity, and so forth – in miniature. This is the basic stuff of market research, and indeed of many social and psychological surveys. But it is not widely done in policy analysis, partly because it assumes in advance that the analyst knows what questions to ask, and partly because it calls for a lot of resources, but mainly because general public opinion is not necessarily the best way for the development or impact of policy to be examined. Samples in policy analysis are much more likely to be *purposive*, or deliberately selected. Examples include key groups (people selected because they perform a particular role in a process), structural samples (people who occupy defined positions and so have a distinct perspective to offer), and stakeholder research (work with people who are directly affected by a policy or engaged with it). Commonly used methods of obtaining data from a purposive sample are correspondence, personal interviews and group discussions. The issues in identifying and consulting with key actors and stakeholders are considered in Chapter five.

Processing and interpreting the data. Books on research methods devote considerable time and space to the issue of how research material should be analysed. The issues are considered further in Chapters Five and Six, which are concerned with intensive and extensive techniques for policy analysis. But this is not a book about research, and there is no attempt here to cover issues like grounded theory or parametric statistics. These are very useful techniques – given the wide range of problems that has to be dealt with, there is often a way to apply them – but they are not central. Policy analysis gathers material for a purpose, and the processing and presentation of data depend strictly on that purpose. This book focuses less on the analysis of research material than on organising the material into the structure required for policy analysis.

Communication

The other main set of skills required in policy analysis relates to communication. Four kinds of communication, apart from those required in research, are particularly important. The first is *work in committees*. The consultant is not expected to engage in argument, because outsiders do not make decisions; contributions in a committee have to be to the point. In academic seminars, students are encouraged to talk, to interact, to work out what they have to say. In a policy committee, the opposite is true. You can often assume that no-one really wants to hear what you have to say if you are not going to agree with them, and even if they do they may have something more interesting to do with their life afterwards. You have to make it brief, and make it count.

The second is *presentation*. Policy analysts have to be able to present material directly and effectively, in a way which is tailored to a specific audience. Often the audience is non-specialised – a community group, a public meeting or elected members. Presentations work best if they use more than one medium – people take in information in different ways, and some will relate better to a slide show or a handout than to the spoken word. Visual materials have to be highly selective for effect; try not to put more than five lines on a slide. Presentations have to be well organised and tightly disciplined. The time allocation allowed is typically somewhere between five and 15 minutes. No-one is going to be more persuaded or more impressed because you went 15 minutes past your allocated time. Learn to deliver your presentations to the minute.

The third is *reporting*. Reports are usually presented in writing. They demand the same skills as academic writing – the selection, ordering and evaluation of material – but the presentation is different:

- Reports need to be concise; all the padding has to go.
- There has to be an executive summary.
- Material has to be sectionalised and numbered, so that committees can refer to specific points.

Reports are not only presented in writing, however. There is often also a verbal component – a formal presentation of results or comments. This calls for a basis of presentational skills, which in most cases now calls for some command at least of computer-generated slides and often of multimedia techniques.

The tests of report writing are simple enough: appropriateness to the audience and fitness for purpose. Clarity is usually (but not always) preferred; academic references should be used very sparingly. Because the report will be the subject of detailed discussion, there should be a means of referring clearly and unambiguously to the main points, such as numbered paragraphs. Reports conventionally should have an executive summary and a clear statement of recommendations. In my teaching, I find that the summary causes students more problems than anything else. They have been trained to write 'introductions' to essays, saying what they are going to do. An executive summary is quite different. It is not a guide to what is coming next. It is a summary: it has to say exactly what is in the report. In principle, it should cover everything that matters. It is there for executive use. The executive summary is there to get decision makers up to speed, and to focus the discussion. One also has to say that it is a rare committee where everyone will have read all the papers before the meeting. (Ideally, a summary should be contained on one side of paper. I was instructed very early on in my career never to base a committee presentation on the expectation that people will turn over the first page. I have found that to be good advice.)

From the point of view of the consultant, the final report may seem crucial. It is the only evidence people will have of the work that has been done. It is how people will judge the work, and it is what the consultant is being paid for. From the point of view of policy, however, the final report is rather less important. It is usually an intermediate stage in the policy process. An excellent report can be left to fester on the shelves, while an inadequate report can still be used as the basis for policy.

These three categories are all aspects of formal communication. The *informal* aspects of communication are also important. It helps if analysts are able to build a rapport with the people they are dealing with. It both improves the flow of information which will be used in the analysis, and it is likely to make the messages that an analyst has to communicate more acceptable.

The role of the policy analyst

Policy analysis is, to some extent at least, a *technical* activity. It involves the application of social science techniques to practice in order to make judgments about policy. Policy analysts are commissioned or requested by policy makers to collate essential information and to provide the basic material for judgments. The analyst is seen as an expert who uses a set of techniques – particularly economics, statistics or other forms of social science – to make an impartial, scientifically valid judgment. The technicalities mean that at times policy analysis is sometimes represented as a technocratic activity. Reading Stokey and Zeckhauser's *A primer for policy analysis*,[4] which introduces policy analysts to simulations, linear programming and decision analysis as part of the 'nuts and bolts' of the subject, it is easy to form the same impression. Some of those techniques are potentially useful: the discussion of queuing in that book should be force-fed to managers of public reception areas everywhere. But, as Wildavsky comments, 'the technical base of policy analysis is weak'.[5] There are too many factors to consider, and too many normative issues, to treat policy analysis as a dispassionate, scientific activity.

Policy analysis is also a *political* activity. Wildavsky goes on: 'unlike social science, policy analysis must be prescriptive; arguments about correct policy ... cannot help but be willful and therefore political'.[6] At the simplest level, policy analysis is political because its subject matter is political: the issues requiring analysis are often contentious and sensitive. This book is less concerned with the technical issues in analysis than with interpretative skills. But policy analysis is also political in a broader sense: the work of policy analysts typically depends on networking, negotiation and diplomacy. In a traditional hierarchy, roles and functions are determined by rules, commands and instructions. Because policy analysis is usually done by someone who is not working in the same team, policy analysts have to negotiate their relationship to policy makers and practitioners. A good general rule, Majchrzak suggests, is that communication with policy makers should start at the beginning of a project and should be maintained all the way through it.[7] Maintaining good relationships is basic to the cooperation needed to do the job. Rhodes commends the diplomatic virtues of 'truthfulness, precision, calm, good temper, patience, modesty and loyalty'.[8] Loyalty is not really relevant for people working from outside the agency, but we might substitute 'trustworthiness'.

Beyond this, policy analysis is an *ethical* activity. Public policy matters, in general, because it makes a difference to people; if it does not, it is using resources which ought to be making a difference somewhere else. Policy analysis is important partly because of its effect on public policy, but also because the actions affect the staff, institutions and users of public services. There are many ethical principles at play – they include issues like democracy, accountability and due process – and many policy analysts will be guided by other values, including commitments to social justice, diversity, liberty or equality. The primary ethical principles which have to be considered by a policy analyst include:

- the moral legitimacy of the policy in relation to the wider society. There are many principles, but the central one is *beneficence* – that policy is supposed to do some good, and not to do harm;
- the responsibilities of the analyst towards the agency – rules like confidentiality, reliability and trust; and
- the individual responsibilities of the analyst – duties to co-workers, and responsibilities not to abuse power or influence (for example, through corrupt practice).

The American Society for Public Administration code of ethics offers guidance intended generally for officials in the public sector; the central principles are to:

- serve the public interest;
- respect the law;
- demonstrate personal integrity;
- promote ethical organisations; and
- strive for professional excellence.[9]

The journal *Policy Evaluation* is more prescriptive: it suggests that policy analysts have a moral responsibility to take account of the side-effects of what they do, to be aware that their recommendations are subject to uncertainty, and to examine the risks they are exposing people to.[10] An activity which is profoundly political and ethical in its character can hardly be constructed in a dispassionate, technical, non-normative framework. There is hardly any activity in public policy which has no ethical dimensions.

The policy analyst is heavily constrained in practice. Policy formation begins from a wide range of sources – ideas, networks, coalitions of interests, agencies, and so forth. Policy analysis, by contrast, begins with a policy that has already been decided and set, usually by someone else. Policy analysts have only a limited scope, and limited power, to make changes in policy. The main way that changes can be brought about is by working through the formal process – pointing to undesired implications for policy, giving advice which favours better policy, and providing a focus for stakeholders who share the analyst's concerns to exercise their influence. In circumstances where the policy analyst actively disagrees with the policy, the options are very limited. In serious cases, such as breaches of ethical codes, this may imply withdrawal from engagement with the policy (which generally means leaving it to someone else who does not have the same reservations), possibly including resignation. This, however, is a counsel of despair, reflecting the inability to change the policy internally, and it removes the prospect of affecting other aspects of policies in the future. Academics sometimes refer to engagement with practice as 'getting your hands dirty'. There is more than one way to read that metaphor. If you really want to avoid political and moral conflicts, you should consider taking up a different line of work.

Exercise

You will find it helpful to familiarise yourself with the kind of work done by policy analysts. Beginning with the site at www.policyhub.gov.uk, go to the bulletin (www.policyhub.gov.uk/bulletins) and review a document given as an example of 'Better Policy Making'.

TWO

The policy process

Policy is a very ambiguous term. In its simplest sense, a policy is a decision about a course of action, but it is also supposed to represent a set of decisions, interrelated and consistent with others. Hogwood and Gunn identify 10 meanings of the term:

- a label for a field of government activity and involvement;
- an expression of the desired state of affairs or general purpose;
- specific proposals;
- the decisions of government;
- formal authorisation;
- a programme of activity – that is, a defined sphere of activity, involving particular measures;
- the output of an agency (what is done);
- outcomes;
- a theory or model – assuming certain results from actions; and
- a process of decision making.[11]

Much of the literature in political science in this field is concerned with the understanding of how policy is made. It addresses questions like, 'who makes the policy?', 'who is the policy for?' and 'who benefits?'. There are several schools of thought for the analysis of policy. Stone argues that policy formation is a process of negotiation or bargaining within the 'polis' or political community. This is essentially an irrational process: negotiation and bargaining depend on the reconciliation of conflicting interests, and people are influenced by many irrational factors, such as concealment, bluff, bargaining, log rolling (trading to get the results one wants), influence, loyalty and so forth.[12] The leading views currently are:

- *Policy networks.* Policy is made through a process of interaction between people in networks, where people negotiate, exchange and share positions. Examples of networks include professional groups, inter-governmental groups and economic producers.
- *Policy streams.* This is a complex view, which holds that policy is influenced by debate in three different areas: the identification of problems, policy debates and the political forum. In each, there is constant debate about policy, and received views about

the agenda and options for development emerge through a process of interaction.

- *Advocacy coalitions.* Policy is seen as the product of a negotiation between different factions, arguing for views and approaches within different policy domains.
- *Rational choice.* This works on the view that policy can be explained through an analysis of rational self-interest.
- *Punctuated equilibrium.* This idea is borrowed from biology. There are long periods of 'equilibrium', when nothing happens, punctuated by sudden and rapid change as the paradigms shift.

Within these competing explanations, Peter John identifies five main types of interpretation:

- institutional – based in the structures and organisations which make policy;
- groups or policy networks – looking at coalitions of interest;
- socio-economic – looking at the predisposing social conditions;
- rational choice – looking for explanations in the self-interest of the parties; and
- ideas-based.[13]

When we analyse policy, we are trying in part to work out what is going on. Policy analysis in political science is mainly concerned with process – why and how decisions are made. That is important both as in intellectual background, and as a way of deciphering what is happening in practice. There are other useful guides to this process, which readers may want to refer to.[14] The main focus of this book, however, is very different. It is concerned less with the formation of policy than with its content – what the policies aim to do, how they are dealt with in practice, and what effect they have. There are times when the aims and effects of policy are unclear, and we are driven back to examining the motives of policy makers. Much more commonly, however, the policy is set, and the task of the policy analyst is not to question why it was ever done, but to see how it operates, and to test whether or not it works.

Policy making

Because so much of the literature about policy analysis derives from the US, the pattern of decision making which is discussed tends to reflect procedures and settings which are very different from the UK. In much of the literature, the typical pattern of policy analysis is based on assessing a 'programme', a stand-alone agency intended to provide a defined service to a target population.[15] Although something of the kind happens in the UK in specific contexts – there has been a blizzard of programmatic development in fields like education, social inclusion and criminal justice – it is not really typical of the policy process in this country. Decisions are generally made within an established structure of authority, and even if policies do not fall directly within the structures of established organisations, such as government departments, local authorities or health boards, there will still be some kind of process or network, like sub-contracting or partnership arrangements, that ties them in to such structures.

The structure of authority

'Authority' means that people have the right to make decisions affecting others. Within organisations, authority is usually invested in a formal body, like a board or council, rather than in individuals. That authority can be delegated to people in specific roles, but it derives from the formal body.

For decisions to be made from the top down, there has to be a hierarchical structure. Within the public sector, this is strongly identified with the idea of a 'bureaucracy'. Decisions in a bureaucracy are made at the highest level, and the task of people at lower levels is to implement the rules. Civil servants in the UK make decisions in the name of their minister; they are anonymous functionaries. In a traditionally run local authority, junior officers have no authorisation to make decisions. Letters are signed in the name of the head of department; in order to trace where the letter actually comes from, the reference code will usually note the initials of the letter's author, and the head of department's signature will be initialled by the person who actually writes the name.

Decisions are not all made from the top down, however; authority in most public sector organisations is delegated or diffused throughout the structure, and policy is made at a range of levels. Professional decision making is very different in structure to bureaucratic approaches. Doctors, the paradigmatic example, are treated as independent professionals, principally accountable to other members of their profession for the standards they maintain. In principle, if not always in practice, no-one tells a medical practitioner what to do; the decision on how to treat a patient is the responsibility or 'clinical judgment' of the doctor. Some policy decisions within the National Health Service (NHS) are made at central level, and some at the level of health authorities, but most have to be negotiated with the medical profession: policy decisions which have originated at the level of the professionals have included centralisation of specialities in large hospitals, the shift against home births, or general practitioner (GP) commissioning (which was initiated by a range of group practices before it became nationally accepted). A number of other professions – social workers, nurses, and teachers – have sought similar status, but operate in practice within the confines of bureaucratic organisations: these are usually referred to as 'semi-professions'.

The third model is the 'manager'. This was imposed in a range of services, most notably in health and education, as part of the 'new public management' of the 1980s and 1990s. Managers have responsibility for the performance of their units, and relative autonomy in the way the units achieve their goals. The role of the manager within the unit is often characterised in terms of 'leadership', a perniciously vague idea which seems to justify any kind of arbitrary authority. In fact, managers are accountable through a set of external constraints. In the private sector, goals are supposed to be understood in terms of profit, which is relatively easy to quantify and measure; in the public sector, goals tend to include a wide range of measures based both on outcomes and on following specified procedures, like 'best value'. This idea of 'management' is strongly linked with government by objectives and targets and the use of performance-linked pay as a reward for successful leadership.[16]

The fourth model is an 'agency' model, based on the distinction between principal and agent. Policy is made by a decision maker (the 'principal'), but the implementation of policy is based on a contract between the policy-making body and someone who carries it out (the agent). Common and Flynn identify four main types of contract. These are:

- *Service contracts.* These are detailed specifications describing the process that will be undertaken.
- *Partnership contracts.* Purchasers and providers collaborate to design a mutual agreement.
- *Service agreements.* Providers are contracted to provide a service, rather than to conduct a specific process. This is commonly used with in-service units and long-standing voluntary organisations.
- *Informal agreements.* Arrangements are made between local managers for ad hoc provision.[17]

In one sense, this model is a hybrid: the ways that different agencies work can include any combination of the other three methods. However, the nature of the contract tends to be strongly geared to the achievement of explicit goals, usually understood in terms of service output – the number of patients treated, the number of clients advised, and so forth. The guidance given to health authorities, for example, allows for three main types of contract:

- block contracts (for provision of a service);
- cost per case (for services to individuals); or
- a combination of cost and volume.[18]

Contracts in the UK generally seem to be made on block contracts with the voluntary sector, but cost per case in the private sector (for example, residential care for elderly people).

This pattern of policy making is a long way from the idea of policy as a system of commands: if policy making has to pass through a series of stages, and it alters at each stage, what comes out may look very different from what happened at the start.[19] Ashworth et al identify five main problems in agency arrangements:

- resistance, where the contracted agencies seek to follow their own agenda;
- ritualistic compliance, where the agenda is distorted by slavish compliance to specified targets;
- performance ambiguity, where because aims are vague, it is not clear what is being done;
- gaps in data, where reporting is made impossible by lack of information; and
- capture, where the principal begins to comply with the agent.[20]

Table 2.1 summarises the main points of the four principal models.

Table 2.1: Systems of authority

	Bureaucrats	**Professionals**	**Managers**	**Agents**
Role	Functionally differentiated administrative tasks	Specialised competence	Leadership	Performance of specified functions
Motivation	Public service	Professional commitment	Incentives	Reward as per contract
Accountability	Responsibility to superiors	Professional standards	Performance criteria	Contract compliance
Decision making	Rule based	Discretion	Quasi-autonomous	Autonomous

There is a fifth model, but it is less important for practice. There are alternative forms of organisation, based on collectivist or cooperative approaches. Some groups reject formal structures. Decisions are made by teams, not by individuals. This model has been influential in feminist groups, like Women's Aid, and it has filtered from there to voluntary groups and some social work teams. These alternatives do not often work well: formal mechanisms make it possible for people to work together despite their differences, and removing the formality often removes essential protections. Charles Handy argues that so much time can be spent negotiating functions and boundaries that the agency can be disabled:

> Dreams without systems (and hard decisions) can become nightmares as the transaction costs of a group exceed its output.[21]

Case study: Social security – the bureaucratic model

The UK social security system is an extreme example of 'top-down' decision making – a bureaucratic system operating on centrally determined rules. In the days of the Poor Law, financial assistance was provided at a local level, and subject to the discretion of the Guardians of the Poor. The system which replaced it was intended to be as different from the Poor Law as possible. Benefits were to be given as of right, and the officials administering the system were not to be given any latitude about the decisions they made.

The system which resulted was consequently as centralised as it possibly could be. In the immediate post-war period, there were two main branches: National Insurance, administered by the Ministry of Pensions and National Insurance, and National Assistance, administered by the National Assistance Board. They were combined into the Department of Social Security in 1966, and the Department of Health and Social Security (DHSS) in 1968. The local offices of the DHSS were administered in accordance with national instructions. Every officer of the DHSS was a civil servant, and subject to the rules of the civil service. All decisions were taken not by individuals, but in the name of the minister. All the actions of the DHSS were governed by the 1911 Official Secrets Act. Civil servants were entitled to be anonymous. The organisation of the offices, and the pattern of service delivery, including forms, filing systems, even the design of office counters, was determined nationally in London. Wherever there were problems which could not be clearly interpreted locally, those problems were referred upwards for decisions. Over time, the combination of decisions, precedents and the need to issue guidance and clarification became progressively more elaborate and complex. This was the most centralised bureaucratic system in the UK; arguably, it was the most centralised system in Western Europe.

The system has undergone successive reforms since, including conversion to delivery by agencies, computerisation, and repeated attempts to change the culture. Claimants are now defined as 'customers', benefit administration has been combined with employment services or shifted away from local agencies. The process of administration, however, remains bureaucratic in form. The task of benefit officers is to operate a huge, complex system as efficiently as possible. Most of the work is done by people working at clerical and executive grades. Claims are not generally dealt with by individual officers, but by a conveyor-belt system known as the 'stream'. Cases are passed to officers with distinct roles – from 'callers' (reception) to relevant benefit sections, with detours for special functions like the Benefit Fraud Inspectorate or the repayments section. The computerisation of most claims means that there are fewer functional divisions within the offices than used to be the case, but there will still be more than one person working on each case, and depending on what needs to be done about the case it will be passed to different parts of the office for processing. The diffusion of responsibilities and functional division of labour reduces the scope for judgment by individuals, and consequently helps to ensure conformity with centrally determined rules.

The bureaucratic approach tends to receive publicity only when it goes wrong – for example, during the Department for Work and Pensions' (DWP) notorious computer crashes. It receives very little attention at all when it does things right. The UK social security system has been destabilised by successive reforms, but at its peak it was remarkably effective. The average office dealt with thousands of claimants every week. Most benefits were processed within a very short period, generally a target of 14 days. This ought to be contrasted with other regimes: in France, the calculation of pensions begins two and a half years before retirement, and is still not paid within the six months after retirement for many claimants. When responsibilities have been transferred from social security offices to other administrations, the other administrations have hardly been able to cope. The transfer of responsibility for Housing Benefits to local authorities, in 1982/83, was described in its day as 'the greatest administrative fiasco in the history of the welfare state'; [22] the local authorities were overwhelmed by the sheer volume of the work. Something similar happened in the development of Child Tax Credit under the aegis of the Inland Revenue:

it took the best part of a year before the Revenue was able to process
many routine claims. What the social security system lost in responsiveness
to individual circumstances, it gained in effective service delivery.

Working in partnership

Many policy decisions in modern government are not made by a
single policy-making body, but by various bodies working together
in partnership. The academic literature has developed the idea of
'policy networks', policy making which depends in principle on the
links between distinct organisations. Policy networks depend on
relationships of reciprocity and interdependence; issues are resolved
through negotiation and diplomacy rather than through the exercise
of authority.[23] 'Partnerships' are formal systems for bringing together
a range of agencies. They take a variety of forms – some are little
more than forums for discussion, while others have a legal status and
substantial budgets in their own right. The principle of partnership is
that various bodies which have a role or interest in relation to an issue
– the 'stakeholders' – work together to achieve their objectives.

Much of the literature on partnerships, and many initiatives, are
concerned with joint working at the level of implementation. But
because the issues depend on policy, irresistibly they have also to be
considered at the level of policy formation. The kinds of joint policy
body that have been made have included:

- attempts at 'joined-up' government, like the Central Policy
  Review Staff of the 1970s or the Social Exclusion Unit in the
  1990s;
- service mergers, like the unification of social work and welfare
  services in the 1960s, or current attempts to merge health and
  social care, or child protection and education; and
- joint priority formation and planning, such as the development
  of community planning partnerships.

The model of partnership dominant in the UK was pioneered in the
1970s. Provision for learning disability (referred to at the time as
'mental handicap') was considered a 'Cinderella' service. It benefited
from two important initiatives: joint planning, undertaken between
health and personal social services, and joint finance, money which
could only be unlocked by services working together on projects.
The subsequent development of services, and the experience that

collaboration is routinely undertaken at every level of the service, owes much to those initiatives.

The experience of the UK has been very different from that of other European countries. In the UK, public services are strongly centred on government, and the relationships which have been most prominent are the relationships between different public services – for example, between health and social work, or social security and employment. In other countries, there has tended to be much more emphasis on the role of different social partners – typically, employers and trades unions, but also commonly including voluntary organisations and mutual funds. That approach is sometimes referred to as 'corporatism'. It ties different organisations together, with the role of the state being, not so much to provide services, as to establish the framework and plan to fill the gaps. Similar approaches are being developed in much of the developing world, as developing countries are required by the International Monetary Fund and World Bank to plan for governance on the basis of collaborative work with social partners.

The difference between the UK and Europe is much less striking than it used to be. Partly this is because of the UK's exposure to European ways of working, but it is also because of the independent recognition of a 'mixed economy' of welfare – that services were not only provided by the state. In the 1980s and early 1990s, the UK government attempted to make the provision of services much more like a private market. The private sector does not need to be 'coordinated'; market economies develop signals through the price mechanism. Several reforms were introduced to make the administration of social services operate more like the management of private enterprise. This approach led to a number of administrative reforms, including:

- in the NHS, the creation of self-governing trusts bidding for patients and resources, and the creation of GP fundholders as 'purchasers';[24]
- in community care, the role of social services departments as the purchaser rather than the provider of care, from multiple providers;[25] and
- in housing, the development of housing associations as a way of breaking up the local authority monopoly of social housing, and the introduction of compulsory competitive tendering for management services.[26]

In principle, these reforms should have made issues of coordination, planning and joint working redundant. In practice, they did the opposite. The market reforms reduced the administration of community care, in particular, to a shambles.[27] Many people working in the field looked to see what they could do, and to do it they drew on the models which they knew to work – often the models of partnership and joint working which people had experienced in the 1970s. The subsequent development of community care was gradually rebuilt, not on market signals, but on partnership, multidisciplinary teamwork, management by objectives, inspection and regulation.

Setting policy

Wherever there are rules, there have to be meta-rules – rules about the rules, which determine how decisions are made, how they are changed, and how they are decided on and enforced. The main conventions governing policy making in Britain are based on government by committee. Decisions which are taken by managers and officials are subject to scrutiny and ratification by a formal system of authority. The conventions include formal constitution of bodies, the recording of decisions (usually through minutes, more rarely through policy books) and the establishment of lines of accountability and reporting back.

Decisions by committees

Decision making by committees has not been examined very closely or systematically. There are various nostrums in the management literature. An example is Parkinson's Law, which suggests that because most people on committees understand small amounts of money better than they understand large ones, the proportion of time spent discussing an issue is likely to be inversely proportional to its importance.[28] Another interesting hypothesis generated by social psychologists concerns the 'shift to risk': that groups have the potential to take decisions which are more risky than any of the members would accept as individuals.[29] (Work on this issue began in the 1960s after the US's bizarre decision to invade Cuba in the Bay of Pigs fiasco.)

Before a decision can be made by a committee, the issue has to reach it. Even if the committee formally makes the rules, there may be an 'executive' – a government, or a civil service – which makes them in practice. Executives often control both agenda and implementation. After a decision, some executives may fail to implement the policy at all: there may effectively be a 'pocket veto' in which policies fall without any overt opposition.

Committee decisions are also strongly influenced by officials. Officials are often accused of pursuing their own agendas: it has been argued that bureaucracies are self-interested.[30] Some are determined to build an empire; some to have an easy life (and some want both at the same time, which is a contradiction in terms). Box 2.1 is not wholly serious, but it has a serious point: officials have a huge potential to shape the agenda. Officials often put forward arguments intended to persuade committees to fund a new project, or to avoid cutting an old one. Anthony and Young list the most common ploys[31]. Most of the titles are self-explanatory: those which are not have a small comment attached.

Box 2.1: How to milk committees for money

Ploys for new programmes
Foot in the door
Hidden ball (hide one programme in another)
Divide and conquer
Distraction
Shell game (hide the key statistics under other ones)
It's free
Implied top-level support
You're to blame
Nothing too good for our people
Keeping up with the Joneses
We must be up to date
If we don't someone else will
Call it a rose
Outside experts

Ploys mainly for managers
Keep them lean and hungry
Productivity cuts
Arbitrary cuts
'I only work here'

Ploys for maintaining or increasing existing programmes
Show of strength
Razzle-dazzle
Delayed buck (let them see the bill afterwards)
Reverence for the past
Sprinkling (add extras to budget estimates to anticipate cuts)

Ploys to resist cuts
Make a study
Gold watch (pick the cuts which antagonise most people – like no gold watch on) retirement
Arouse client antagonism
Witches and goblins (scare them)
We are the experts
End run (go outside normal channels)

Source: R Anthony, D Young, 1984, cited in C Clark, I Lapsley, 1996, *Planning and costing community care*, London: Jessica Kingsley Publishers.

Decisions by officials

The decision of a committee is not the end of the process; it is only a stage on the way. The lines of policy formation are not always clear: some agencies distinguish policy from 'management practice', which effectively are rules devolved by management. Wherever there are rules, officials have to use their judgment to determine whether or not a case fits the rules: judgment is inevitable. Where there are no rules or policy, officials have to use *discretion*. Discretion is not the same thing as judgment.[32] Judgments have to be made because someone has to apply the rules, and every decision about rules is a judgment. Discretion happens where there are no pre-existing rules; it is about the decisions which fill in the gaps. Discretion is not inevitable, but it is difficult for a policy-making body to legislate for every contingency, and this makes discretion difficult to avoid. The same principle applies throughout the public service. There are the rules that are made by policy makers, the rules that are made for people working in practice, and, in many cases, the rules that the officers at the coalface make for themselves. Lipsky refers to the formation of policy by officers in contact with the public as 'street level bureaucracy'.[33]

But there are many other reasons why officials might want, or even need to make rules. Some of the rules relate to simple, practical problems, like the management of dates: benefits offices use the first letter of a person's surname to divide the workload between sections. Some reflect practical constraints. I used to work in the allocation of council housing, where there was a huge difference between the formal rules and 'management practice'. Because there are different sizes of household, and because most people prefer some areas over others, most housing providers run multiple lists, classified by size and type of property and location. This is often not stated in the formal policy, but, for any provider managing a diversified housing stock, it would be extraordinary if it did not happen. And there are 'service ideologies' – linked sets of values, beliefs and approaches, which emerge in different services.[34] Policy is not only about the issues that are formally decided on and set down.

Beyond the issues of practice, there are several examples of policy being made from the 'bottom up'. Officials try to work out practical ways of responding to issues; their practice is imitated by others; the approach is taken up by decision makers at local or national level; the practice becomes general policy. Examples include:

- the introduction of deterrent workhouses, pioneered in Nottinghamshire in the 1820s – George Nicholls, the overseer at the workhouse in Southwell, became a Poor Law Commissioner on the strength of his work;
- the development of 'breakfast clubs' in schools, which became national policy after several years of local initiatives;
- the use of short-term loans to help families in need, developed under powers made available to social workers in 1963[35] and later incorporated into the Social Fund; and
- the development of GP commissioning within the NHS, which grew from voluntary cooperation between practices for the purchasing of services.[36]

Case study: Policy for homeless people

Decision making is not necessarily 'top down' or 'bottom up'; it depends on a mix of different influences. Policy is often seen as stemming from legislation, particularly the 1977 Housing (Homeless Persons) Act, but this is only half right. Homelessness is an area where many of the rules come from official practice rather than national policy.

Homeless people were dealt with under the Poor Law until 1948. The 1948 National Assistance Act, which abolished the Poor Law, required local authorities to develop schemes to provide for people in the event of homelessness. Ministers were given extensive powers to impose schemes, but these were never used. Some authorities ignored the legislation altogether; some developed their own practices, giving some homeless people priority while denying access to others. In some cases, families were separated, or children were taken into care. *Cathy come home*, a BBC play based on the situation, raised national concern, and prompted the foundation of Shelter, the national campaign for homeless people.

In 1971, a Shelter report made the case, persuasively, that the law was being flouted.[37] The response of the Conservative government, in order to remove any doubt, was to abolish the law: the 1972 Local Government Act converted the duty to rehouse homeless people into a power to rehouse. The Labour government, elected in 1974, pledged to restore the duty, but it did not do so. Instead, it issued a circular, or formal advice, to local authorities to rehouse homeless people. It confined the scope of that circular to priority groups – mainly families with children and vulnerable people. (This approach was based in the practice which had developed in some London boroughs.[38] Single people and childless couples were excluded partly because it was considered that the private rented sector could provide for their needs, and partly because accommodation was defined as being for families.) When the Housing (Homeless Persons) Act was passed in 1977, it also confined the principal obligations to those priority groups.

The legislation on homeless people represented an uneasy compromise between the general principle of rehousing homeless people, pressure from local authorities, and the practice of the time. In recognition of strong political opposition, the 1977 Act introduced a test of 'intentionality': people in priority groups who were intentionally homeless would be entitled only to temporary, not to permanent, accommodation. The Act offered fewer rights to homeless people, then, than the previous legislation. But the rights were in a more enforceable form. A long series of legal cases went to court, not because of uncertainty about the law – the Act, as these things go, was remarkably clearly written – but because of determined resistance from some local authorities. The courts usually decided, more or less, that the Act really meant what it said. Current reforms mean that the distinctions between priority groups and judgments about intentionality are, at last, being removed.

The core problem here is not the practice or attitude of housing providers; it is scarcity. There have been declining numbers of affordable houses and reduced social housing stocks. The contemporary situation, by comparison with the 1970s, is less pressured for families, but worse for single people. Another trend over time has been the opening out of large differences in local conditions, largely reflecting a maldistribution of social housing nationally. There are some places where affordable housing is virtually unobtainable, while others have substantial surpluses of 'difficult to let' housing. Currently, there are over 192,000 people on housing lists in Scotland, and only 40,000 properties a year are available for letting;[39] at that rate, the mean waiting time is five years, although the mismatch of applications and the available stock means, more realistically, that some people will never be housed. The pressure on local authority housing was, and is, unmanageable.

The tension between national policy and local practice reflects, then, some genuine problems. In some areas, local authorities were resistant to rehousing people on the basis of need. The legislation was not a major social advance, but at least it helped to redress the balance. This leaves, however, the question of what happens in the places where the law cannot be complied with.

Rules that cannot be obeyed tend to be bent or broken. Typical administrative responses to unmanageable pressures are:

- *deterrence* – making it difficult for people to gain access to services. This is a common administrative refuge. Most officials seem to disapprove of deterrence, but when push comes to shove, and they are denied either resources or legitimate rationing systems, they do it.
- *delay*. Many local authorities have used temporary accommodation, particularly accommodation in bed and breakfast accommodation, as a staging post before permanent rehousing. This practice is generally disapproved of – it is unsatisfactory for families, and massively expensive.
- *taking restrictive interpretations of rules*. One common restrictive interpretation is to say that homeless families should receive one offer of accommodation, with no choice, because at the point where they have accommodation they cease to be homeless.
- *ignoring inconvenient rules*. The law does not say that people who are intentionally homeless should not be helped. On the contrary, they are entitled to advice, assistance and temporary accommodation. This provision has been more honoured in the breach than the observance.
- *inventing new rules*. There is nothing in the law which says that people will only be accepted as homeless if there is a court order for their eviction, that people under 18 cannot have a tenancy, or that students are not eligible for rehousing. These are all invented rules, used either to deter people or to limit the demand.

It can be difficult to distinguish policy from administration, or to work out the difference between interpreting rules and breaking them. In principle, it should be true that legislation determines policy, and policy determines administration. In practice, the reverse may also be true.

The policy cycle

If policy can be made at different levels, and a range of actors play a part in developing policies, the result is unlikely to take the form of a neat, ordered structure. Policy is difficult to read, in more than one sense of that term. It is often difficult to find out what a policy is, who has made decisions, and where a policy has come from. By the same token, it can be difficult to reform policy, or to manage change.

There have been many schemes intended to impose some order on the process. Some agencies work to strict timetables for policy review. Figure 2.1 is from a work intended to recommend a structure of

Figure 2.1: The policy cycle

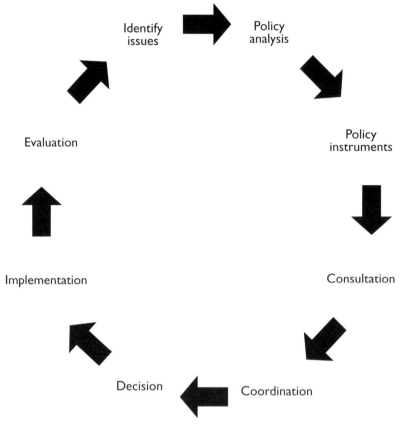

Source: P Bridgman and G Davis, 1998, *Australian policy handbook*, Sydney: Allen and Unwin.

decision making for Australian policy makers. It identifies eight main stages in the policy process.[40]

The idea of the policy cycle is based on a sequence of ordered stages. This offers policy makers a useful checklist, but in real life policy is not likely to be as well ordered as this suggests. Policy instruments are likely to be refined and developed as time goes on; consultation may not go to schedule; coordination and partnership work is likely to be continuous; policy analysis can be undertaken at any stage of the process.

The purpose of outlining a policy cycle is that many of these stages come 'lexically' before others – that is, it makes sense to do one thing before another. It is often appropriate to ask, 'shouldn't we be doing this first?', where 'this' might be policy analysis before identifying methods, consultation before a decision, implementation before evaluation, or evaluation before new policy.

Exercise

Review some recent minutes of the deliberations of a local authority (you can quickly find a set by a search using Google on 'minutes gov.uk'). What further information would be needed to translate decisions as recorded into a comprehensible account of the policy which has been authorised?

THREE

Strategic policy making

The structure of a policy analysis

The idea of the policy cycle is based on a 'rational' model of policy making, sometimes called the 'rational-comprehensive' model. Rational decision making follows a process which allows the examination of each stage in a policy, and feedback from results into further decision making. The basic stages look something like this:

1. *Assessment of the environment.* Decisions have to be taken in the light of existing situations.
2. *The identification of aims and objectives.* Aims and values have to be identified and established as criteria by which decisions can subsequently be evaluated.
3. *Consideration of the alternative methods which are available.* Different ways of achieving the aims and objectives are identified. This is a question of what is possible.
4. *Selection of methods.* The possible consequences of all the possible methods are judged against the aims and objectives in order to decide their likely effectiveness. The selection of particular methods of working is then guided by consideration of efficiency and practical constraints.
5. *Implementation.* The policy is put into practice.
6. *Evaluation.* The consequences of policy are monitored, and fed back into a re-assessment of the environment – at which point the process begins again.[41]

The rational model is stated differently in different places: some presentations cover as few as four stages (aims, methods, implementation and outcomes), while others have ten or more (context, aims, objectives, goals, methods, predictions of consequences, selection, implementation, monitoring, evaluation and feedback). The version given in the Treasury's *Green Book*, which it calls the ROAMEF cycle, covers:

1. a *rationale* for policy;
2. identification of *objectives*;
3. *appraisal* of options;

4. implementation and *monitoring*;
5. *evaluation*; and
6. *feedback*.[42]

This is expressed differently, but at its root it is much the same thing as the rational model: it involves an ordered progression from aims, to methods, to implementation, and to evaluation. The main difference from the first list given is the substitution of 'rationale' for 'evaluation of the environment'. Reference to a 'rationale' lumps together several issues which ought to be distinct – the justification for a policy, general aims and values, the evaluation of the environment, and the reason for selecting different methods and approaches. In the chapters which follow, these are dealt with sequentially.

The advantage of the rational model is that it makes it possible to discuss policy in a way that is systematic and explicit. But the model has been heavily criticised. The first problem is that it demands more of policy makers than may be practical or feasible; the examination of alternative approaches and their consequences is time-consuming, expensive and often speculative. Second, it fails to address issues of conflict. Conflicts in values and intentions, and conflicts relating to administrative method, have to be negotiated and compromises arrived at. Whether or not it is intended to do so, the rational model tends to give the impression that there is a smooth progression from one stage of policy making to the next. Third, it ignores the realities of policy making. Policy makers learn as they go along, and even if they do not learn, the things they do are likely to be changed by the experience of doing them. The process of implementation itself changes (or deflects) the impact of policy.

The main alternative to the rational model has been 'incrementalism'. Lindblom argues that decision makers have to 'muddle through'; it is easier in practice to agree methods than it is to agree aims, and in practice ends and means are chosen simultaneously.[43] In Lindblom's view, decisions are primarily an outcome of power relationships, and only a limited range of options will be considered, but the process is one of constant refinement and compromise. He refers to the process of mediation as 'partisan mutual adjustment'.[44] Outcomes are examined, then, by a very different process from the 'rational' model; the process is one of experimentation, review of the consequences that are perceived as important, adjustment and compromise, and coping with problems rather than solving them.

Although incrementalism is often a realistic description of the process of policy making, it suffers from a central problem: an incremental strategy, proceeding by negotiation and compromise, tends to reflect the structure of power and to close off certain options for change. Leach defends the rational model on the basis that it can be seen as a set of prescriptions for policy, rather than a description of what really happens; it does not have to be done perfectly, and – far from concealing conflicts – it can be used to make assumptions and values explicit.[45]

The reason for beginning with the rational model is not that it works as a description of policy: it doesn't. Nor is it a prescription; it is missing several important issues, like legitimacy, accountability and democracy. There is a strong argument for having public and user participation at every level, and the rational model does not apply that as a test. It is not necessarily the best way to tackle a problem – that might well be to do something, rather than to talk about it – although it may help avoid some of the most obvious mistakes. What the rational model does do is to lay out a framework for the structured analysis of policy. The stages proposed in the rational model differ in different formulations. If you work as a policy analyst, you will need to appraise policy in a systematic way. To do that, you will need to consider most of these stages – at the very least, context, aims, methods and implementation – and as a broad proposition you will need to do it in something like that order. The model works, then, as a checklist. The longer versions of the checklist add a few extra stages to the core – for example, goal setting, constraints, monitoring procedures and evaluation – but it is not a bad idea to keep those in mind.

The rational model was developed mainly with policy formation in mind, rather than policy analysis, and there are some significant differences between them. Policy analysis begins with an established policy, not with a blank sheet. The purpose of the exercise is usually to determine whether the policy is working. That means that the first step in a policy analysis is usually some consideration of the aims of policy; those aims set the terms, and determine the scope, of the assessment. The order the rest of the book follows, then, is not quite the order of either version of the rational model. The stages are:

- identifying aims, values and goals;
- assessing the environment;
- identifying methods;
- selecting methods;
- analysing implementation; and
- evaluation.

These stages can be difficult to separate in practice. Working out what the aims are, what the criteria should be, and whether the problem being analysed is really the problem stated, all tend to come together at the start of the process.[46] Analysing the environment, and engaging with stakeholders, is difficult to do without considering the issues of implementation or the effects of policy. Reviewing the issues in stages is artificial, but it makes it possible to distinguish some of the elements of policy.

Strategic planning

The rational model lies at the root of a range of planning methods used in public sector agencies. The basis of planning usually depends on four main stages:

- the establishment of aims – often a mission, or general statement of aims, backed up by other subordinate aims;
- the establishment of outcomes – goals or targets by which the success or failure of the methods can be established;
- the identification of the methods; and
- the precision of a plan of work by which the methods will be implemented.

Suppose, for example, that the plan to be developed is a plan to respond to a particular issue, like domestic violence. The Home Office guidance on strategy in this area[47] suggests three main aims:

- prevention and early intervention;
- protection and justice;
- support for victims.

Within each category, it suggests some illustrative methods and approaches, including for example:

- *prevention*
  - changing public attitudes
  - working with young people
  - giving information to potential victims
- *protection*
  - improving collaboration between agencies
  - access to justice
- *support for victims*
  - developing advocacy services
  - building on existing support networks.

This structure may seem restrictive, but these are guidelines, not rules. There is scope within it for considerable flexibility and imagination.

The examples given in the report include work not just with the obvious groups, like solicitors and women's refuges, but with taxi drivers and locksmiths. This kind of structure has two main purposes. First, it identifies the contribution of each measure to the whole. Second, it helps to point to the gaps – the areas where too little is being done.

The principles of strategic planning are now widely accepted and applied. They have become the norm in central and local government in Britain. In the process of 'community planning', local authorities and their partners are invited to lay out a general approach, or 'vision'; to identify key themes for action; and to devise an action plan, including the key actors engaged in realising the policy and suggesting target outcomes. Community planning is more, however, than the development of strategies for action; it involves a partnership approach. The scope of a community plan is not confined to local government; it implies a commitment to work with others, usually including other government agencies, and sometimes (if more rarely) extending into cooperation with independent groups, voluntary agencies and representative organisations.

The same principles apply in other parts of the world. The European Union has required strategic plans from each of its member states on issues like social inclusion and employment. Developing countries have been required by international organisations, including the International Monetary Fund and the World Bank, to create Poverty Reduction Strategy Papers, or PRSPs. The papers are based on five main principles:

- the plans would be country driven, rather than set by the international organisations;
- they would be results-oriented, setting targets;
- they would take a long-term perspective;
- they would be comprehensive, dealing with poverty as a multi-dimensional problem; and
- they would be based in partnerships, with extensive participation from civil society.[48]

It is very difficult to say whether this will deal with the issues of poverty more effectively, or lead to a better response, than other methods might. Despite the name, PRSPs do not have much to do with poverty. What the method does do is to change the way that governments work. Countries are being encouraged to develop systematic planning, monitoring and evaluation of their actions. The main emphasis in most PRSPs falls on planning, partnership and participation. Governments are expected to plan their methods of governance explicitly, they have to consult with a range of partners, and they have to review and monitor outcomes. These are the same approaches as those expected of governments in developed economies.

Case study: Developing an anti-poverty strategy

Many local authorities in Britain have developed anti-poverty strategies, but the range of policies included in such strategies tends to be limited: it reflects a general perception of the limitations of local authority services, and the restricted scope for innovation. Donnison identifies six main categories:

1. reduced charges or costs for poor people;
2. improved access to services, including welfare rights;
3. developing opportunities for participation;
4. creating opportunities for employment;
5. policies on safety and crime; and
6. urban regeneration.[49]

There is scope, however, for a different, more wide-ranging view of an anti-poverty strategy: a strategy concerned more generally with the role of a local authority in relation to its population.

In 1999 I was seconded by my university to work as Anti-Poverty Strategy Coordinator commissioned for Dundee Council. Despite the wonderfully elaborate job title, the role was hemmed in with limitations. As an outsider, working on a short fixed-term contract, I could not impose a policy, or see it through. A large part of the work consisted, not of writing a strategy, but of a process of negotiation: discussing with officials and community activists what they hoped to see included, giving them ownership of aspects of policy, committing them to the process. The approach to developing an anti-poverty strategy was conservative: much of the stress fell, not on developing new policies, but on identifying and incorporating existing contributions. Any new proposals had to be incremental and marginal if they were to stand a chance of being implemented.

The process of developing strategic aims began, in one sense, from a theoretical position: that poverty is multi-faceted, and that its dimensions include needs, economic and social. That implied three basic categories:

- meeting needs;
- improving economic position;
- social inclusion.

Within each category, there are several subordinate categories. The plan is detailed in Table 3.1.

Table 3.1: Anti-poverty strategy

1. Meeting needs
1.1 Delivering services which meet needs
    1.1a   Providing services for older people
    1.1b   Providing services for children and families
    1.1bi   Providing services for single parents
    1.1c   Providing services for people who are chronically sick or disabled
    1.1d   Providing services for unemployed people
    1.1e   Providing services for homeless people
1.2 Targeting resources
    1.2a   Redistributing resources to those who are poorest
    1.2b   Providing general services for groups of people who are particularly likely to suffer from poverty
    1.2c   Ensuring that general services are available to those who are poorest
    1.2d   Providing services specifically for people in poverty
1.3 Indirect provision: directing people towards resources and services available from other services
    1.3a   Enabling people to meet their own needs
    1.3b   Information and advice
    1.3c   Helping people to obtain resources through representation, aid and advocacy

2. Improving economic position
2.1 Economic development
    2.1a   Economic development in general
    2.1b   Economic development of poorer areas
2.2 Employment
    2.2a   Providing employment
    2.2b   Developing employment prospects
    2.2c   Protecting people who are marginally employed
2.3 Mobilising resources
    2.3a   Obtaining external funding or grant aid
    2.3b   Maximising personal income
    2.3c   Securing resources in kind

continued

Table 3.1: Anti-poverty strategy contd.../

3. Social inclusion

3.1 Developing participation in society

    3.1a   Developing personal capacity, interests and opportunities

    3.1b   Integrating the person in a supportive social environment

    3.1c   Involving people in social and cultural activities

    3.1d   Preventing factors which make people vulnerable to poverty

    3.1e   Ensuring safety and security

3.2 Empowerment

    3.2a   Participation in decision making

    3.2b   Collective action with others

    3.2c   Engagement in the political process, and representation of interests

3.3 Developing the communities on which inclusion depends

    3.3a   Developing and extending social networks within communities

    3.3b   Developing skills and competences within communities

    3.3c   Developing and regenerating the infrastructure on which communities depend

Source: Dundee City Council, 1999, *Anti-poverty strategy*, Dundee: Dundee City Council, www.dundeecity.gov.uk/publications/antipov.pdf, Reproduced with permission.

The categories which were used in most cases reflected the pattern of existing policies. Services for children and families might have been dealt with in other ways, but had to be included as a category because of the city's flagship programme for children and families. Ensuring safety and security, one of Donnison's categories of anti-poverty policy,[50] might have been identified as a category in advance, but in fact it was identified as a heading three weeks before the finalisation of the report, because only then had returns from officers identified enough areas of activity for it to be included.

The hierarchical structure serves two main purposes. First, it makes it possible to see the relationships between specific actions and the overall strategy. Second, the categorisation identifies both objectives where there was a great deal of activity (such as employment training) and others where there were gaps (such as provision for single parents or people who were unable to work).

There were three types of recommendation in the strategy document. First, there were proposals developed from particular constituencies – policies which stakeholders wished to see emphasised or developed. Second, there were proposals arising from gaps identified in the process of developing the strategy. These included provisions for single parents, unemployed people, and a review of the distributive implications of some of the council's policies. Third, there were proposals to make the strategy work in the future. These were:

- a review of the council's information on poverty;
- procedures for the monitoring and reporting of progress on the anti-poverty strategy; and
- the introduction of a system for monitoring the implications of policy developments for poverty.

Much of this did not happen, and consequently the impact of the policy was greatly limited.

Understanding the relationship between plans

The plans related to specific issues are only part of a larger picture. Planning in these terms has become so widely accepted, and so generally practised, that public sector agencies are not dealing with a single, rational plan. Many local authorities in the UK have some 30 to 50 inter-related plans, developed over a number of years; some have more. In Scotland, for example, North Ayrshire Council lists 35 related strategies and plans in its community plan; Falkirk Council lists 59. The relationship between these plans depends on the identification of a structure which links and unites them. Typically there will be at least three levels of planning:

1. strategy, identifying overarching aims and objectives, a range of issues and fields of operation;
2. planning for fields of operation, identifying for each area of work how services will operate and policies will function; and
3. policy, where specific policies are devised.

These methods are now widely used in local government, and have accelerated with the introduction of 'community planning', undertaken by partnerships of local authorities, public sector agencies and some independent organisations.

Strategic plans. Strategic plans provide a framework for other plans and policies. The term implies that there is a hierarchy of policies. The strategic plan establishes the general principles and identifies a range of contributory policies. A coherent strategy should identify both the relationship of policies to each other, and their relationship to the strategy overall. The primary purpose of setting out this hierarchy is to make the structure and relationships between different policies visible. It becomes possible to identify not only what the objectives are, but where they fit in relation to other policies. The case study in this chapter of an anti-poverty strategy gives an example of a hierarchically ordered plan.

The rational approach on its own helps to make policy explicit, systematic, consistent with its aims, and considered. The combination with strategic planning should make it possible to identify contradictions between policy. It is fairly common, for example, for local authorities to have both an environmental policy, emphasising conservation and sustainability, and an economic policy, emphasising growth and development. These do not have to conflict with each other, but if the policies are not cross-referred, there is a danger that they might. Putting both of them in the framework of a strategic plan is a way of checking that they do not. In the same way, a strategic framework should identify the points where policies duplicate each other, and gaps in coverage – areas where there are objectives which are not covered by any of the contributory policies. If a strategic plan is properly constructed, it should provide a clear map of the relationships between policies. Reading from the top down, it should be possible to identify the aims of the plan overall, the fields of operation where it applies, and the policies that are intended to implement it. Reading from the bottom up, it should be possible for everyone working in a service to see what the structure plan is asking of them, how their service fits the structure, and what the relationship is between different branches.

Fields of operation. There tend to be many policies which have to be reconciled. In practice, there tend to be many more than two plans to consider. The plans cover:

- general issues and areas, like 'the environment', 'community safety', or 'economic development';
- plans for the delivery of services, like education or social work, or for parts of services, like waste disposal or city centre management; and
- cross-cutting issues and problems, like 'children and young people' or 'drug and alcohol abuse'.

The structure of policy within each of these fields generally follows the basic model of rational planning: it includes statements of aims, methods, anticipated outcomes and a plan of work. Each plan needs, however, to refer back to the aims and objectives of the structure plan, to ensure that the role and approach is fully compatible with other plans on other issues.

Specific policy By the time plans have been established for an overall strategy, the aims of policy should have been clearly established. Planning for specific policy is consequently more circumscribed, and tends to call for only the later part of the rational model. This is usually represented in 'action plans'. An action plan consists, in its simplest form, of a description of methods, targets and a timetable for action, including identification of the persons or bodies responsible for each action. The idea of an action plan is linked to project management. In its detailed form, project management will break down complex activities into a series of defined tasks, specify exactly who is responsible for each task, and establish a timescale within which the task is to be done. In strategic plans, the specified actions are commonly framed fairly loosely, but the basic elements are the same: identification of tasks, timetables for the tasks to be completed, and allocation of responsibilities. Taken in combination with the other elements of strategic planning, there will also be a statement of purpose and criteria established by which the effectiveness of the action can be judged.

At the same time, the relationship between action plans and strategic planning is often unclear. Part of the problem is that the development of services is often incremental, rather than rational. Strategic planning tends to be undertaken after services are in place, in the hope of adding a rationale to a range of services which are complex and lacking in overall coherence. Some services do not fit the rationale, and either the services get left out, or the rationale has to be stretched. Some plans become a shopping list of services. Others are decorated, like an Xmas tree, with little illustrations of policies which happened to be on hand. They may not belong together, but they add to the brightness and colour of the occasion.

Developing strategic plans

Strategic plans identify the most important issues in a range of contributory plans. In principle, they come at the top of the hierarchy: the proposals in a strategy should guide decisions made at lower levels.

In practice, this is rarely what happens. Most public sector agencies have existed for years. They have developed policies, practices and strategies of their own. The growth of rational–comprehensive methods has encouraged people to be more explicit about their aims, methods and outcomes; it has not led to them making policy for the first time. When overarching strategies are being developed, like national action plans or community planning, they are generally built on the foundations of existing policy and practice.

In almost every case, then, developing a strategy has to be an interactive process. It begins with discussion and identification of the work undertaken by different people. It includes a range of activities. The principles which are adopted as part of strategic planning are not simply prescriptive – saying what ought to happen; they are also descriptive – saying what does happen. Some principles lend themselves to a diverse, inclusive approach, and some do not. The idea of 'social inclusion' works very well on this model, because it can draw in contributions made from a range of sources, and each service, programme and project can be argued to add to the whole. (This is one of the reasons why the principle has gained such favour in the European Union, which is trying to present the disparate work of many national governments as part of a cohesive European effort.) By contrast, 'social justice' is much more difficult to represent in this way, because justice depends, to a much greater degree than inclusion, on consistent treatment of people in similar circumstances.

Some problems are predictable. One is that officers are likely to resent directions from on high, and may be defensive or dismissive. One of the classic works on this field, *Dilemmas of social reform*, describes how an enthusiastic agency is appointed to coordinate the efforts of many other agencies and the coordinators find, to their astonishment, that the other agencies do not appreciate being coordinated.[51] Another problem is that there are likely to be inconsistencies between strategic objectives at different planning levels. Where there are inconsistencies, it is not clear that the strategy will be given priority. Officials tend to be committed to the plans and programmes that are closest to their work, not to grand designs. If, for example, a Drug and Alcohol Action Team have drawn up a plan which says that they are committed to helping people with drug-related problems in the community, and the community plan says that firm action will be taken to preserve community safety by ensuring strict policing and condemnation of anti-social behaviour related to drug abuse, there is a potential contradiction between the two approaches. The first line of defence will be to say that there is no actual inconsistency between the two principles – helping people with addictions reduces the risk to the public. The second line of defence will be to refer to other plans, such as national plans on drug and alcohol abuse, which have a different emphasis. Finally, in practice, the team can largely ignore the community plan, which can be assumed to be aimed at other workers, and get on with meeting the need. Strategy making, like most other policy making, is a political activity. It calls for negotiation and brokering, and it needs different stakeholders to take responsibility for taking actions forward.

If strategy making is a political activity, the pretence of 'rationality' may seem hard to justify. What, then, is the point? There are still strong arguments for making policy explicit, for exploring the potential for policies to reinforce each other, to address contradictions, and to identify gaps. This is what the rational model is good for. That is why the model has had such an impact.

Case study: Gender mainstreaming

Kirsteen Davidson and Paul Spicker
Mainstreaming is an alternative approach to strategy formation, emphasising principles and procedures rather than specific identification of aims, goals or methods. It is intended to be a process by which equal opportunities principles, strategies and practices can be fully integrated into the work of government and public bodies. The United Nations Beijing Declaration and Platform for Action argued that:

> Governments and other actors should promote an active and visible policy of mainstreaming a gender perspective in all policies and programmes so that, before decisions are taken, an analysis is made of the effects on women and men respectively.[52]

The European Commission adopted gender mainstreaming after the 1997 Treaty of Amsterdam. The Commission's work, particularly in relation to its Structural Fund programmes, has been influential in driving forward the mainstreaming agenda at local and regional levels. In the UK, the work of the Equal Opportunities Commission, the creation of specialist government units and ministries, and the development of the government's cross-cutting modernisation agenda,[53] have all played key roles in promoting the equality mainstreaming agenda, while the devolved Parliament in Scotland and the assemblies in Wales and Northern Ireland have all formally adopted an equalities mainstreaming approach.

There are three main elements in mainstreaming:
- mainstreaming *principles*;
- mainstreaming *systems* (such as strategies, structures or processes); and
- mainstreaming *tools* (such as monitoring arrangements, impact assessments and education and training).[54]

Mainstreaming works partly by encouraging or requiring agencies to take gender issues into account, and partly by creating an opportunity for advocates of equal opportunities to raise gender issues legitimately within the procedures.

Applying the criteria usually applied to strategic planning, the process of mainstreaming has some important deficiencies. It begins with an identification of principles, but principles are not necessarily tied to methods. There are no identifiable goals, and no clear criteria for evaluation. The influence on practice can, however, be difficult to identify. The Scottish Parliament has adopted the following measures as part of its strategy to mainstream equality:

- The Standing Orders of the Parliament direct that all Executive Bills coming before it must include an equal opportunities impact assessment.
- An Equal Opportunities Committee of the Scottish Parliament has been established.
- An Equality Unit has been established within the Scottish Executive. Its remit includes the development of a mainstreaming awareness strategy, a training and development strategy, securing improvements in equalities information to inform the development of equal opportunities impact assessments, and the development of monitoring and evaluation tools.
- A mainstreaming 'checklist' has also been developed for use by Elected Members when considering policy.

This does not link the selection of methods to the aims. It is a list of measures rather than a systematic approach.

Evaluations of mainstreaming have tended to focus on two main questions:

- Have agencies adopted the procedures associated with mainstreaming?[55]
- Have policies been adopted which reflect concerns and issues about gender?[56]

These are both legitimate areas of concern, but something is missing. We also need to ask: has the process of mainstreaming itself made a difference to the character of the policies adopted? If it has not, the value of mainstreaming is unlikely to be more than symbolic.

Exercise

Critically review a Poverty Reduction Strategy Paper from www.imf.org/
external/np/prsp/prsp.asp

FOUR

Aims, values and goals

Policies are usually associated with objectives. In planning documents, objectives are of two main types: aims and goals. Statements of objectives are also complemented by statements of a mission or purpose, and statements of values. These terms are not fixed, and sometimes they are used interchangeably, but the types of things which are referred to are reasonably distinct.

- A *mission* (or vision) is a statement of purpose. It is, then, a general statement of aims and values which comes before any specific policy has been determined. Examples of mission statements might be 'promoting a knowledge economy', 'developing sustainable communities' or 'helping people to have a healthier old age'. A mission could also be referred to as an aim, but the important issue is that it is generalised and at a higher level than specific service objectives.
- *Values* are an important dimension in statements of objectives, but they are not always identified explicitly. Values are moral principles or norms. They can be used positively, to lead policy in a particular direction, or negatively, to forestall certain options. Positive examples might be promoting 'health' or 'social inclusion'; negative examples might be 'confidentiality' (which is a statement of how information will not be used) or 'prudence' (a commitment not to do anything rash).
- *Aims* are what a policy is supposed to achieve. General purposes have to be 'operationalised'. That means that they have to be translated into terms which can be realised, or put into practice. If, for example, the mission is to promote a knowledge economy, the aims might be to increase the proportion of people attending higher education and the proportion of those in work who undertake training and knowledge-based staff development.
- *Goals* are specific objectives, identifying the precise outcome which a policy is meant to achieve. (Some people will use the term 'objectives' only to refer to goals.) Goals are also called targets. They have two purposes: they are both a practical outcome, and a test of whether the aims are being achieved. (It is possible for targets to be set which have a desirable practical

outcome – for example, building a creche – which have nothing to do with the aim. Conversely, it is possible to have targets set which reflect the aim – like 'improving the image of the city' – but which have no means of being evaluated.)

The mission

'Missions' go beyond statements of values. For many agencies, their 'mission' is a statement of their role and function, including methods as well as aspirations. In practice, this tends to be less a device for making policy than a form of public relations or advertising, although it can also be used as a way of offering 'leadership' to employees who are otherwise baffled by the organisation they are part of.

Here, by way of illustration, are some mission statements for ministries of health.[57]

- The UK's Department of Health's aim is 'to improve the health and well-being of people in England'. (Scotland, Wales and Northern Ireland are served by their own agencies.)
- For the US Department of Health and Human Services, it is 'Protecting the health of all Americans and providing essential human services, especially for those unable to help themselves'.
- The Department of Health and Children in Ireland aims 'to protect, promote and restore the health and well-being of people by ensuring that health and well-being are planned, managed and delivered to achieve measurable health and social gain and provide the optimum return on resources invested'.

The third of these statements is much more specific about methods and constraints. This does not look quite so good on letterheads, but it may be more appropriate to the organisation; if organisations do not have specific tasks to perform, it is not always clear why they exist.

There is room to debate whether these mission statements are helpful. They can be so wide that anything could be included. And they may not reflect what the organisation really does at all. The UK's Department of Health is not concerned with the general well-being of the population. It does not deal with issues that are essential to people's welfare, like education, housing, income, family relationships or culture. In so far as these are the concern of government, they are the responsibility of other departments. Beyond that, it is fairly debatable whether the Department of Health is actually about health. For most of the last 60 years, it has been concerned with medical services, which are important, but quite different. If we wanted better health, then smoking less, eating better and tackling poverty would be much more effective than providing medical care. The provision of medical care is done for other reasons: first, to offer social protection, or basic cover for the medical problems that people might experience, and second, to offer continuing care for people who need certain types of support. Possibly the mission statement is just missing the point. Possibly it is a statement of what the service ought to be doing, instead of what it is doing – there have been many attempts in recent years to refocus services on health improvement or health promotion, rather than medical care alone. Possibly, too, it is making a claim – that politicians should keep their hands off the service because without it there will be no health or well-being. It is not clear that the mission statement is directly translated into policy or practical action.

This judgment may seem dismissive, and to some extent it is. That is a cause for regret, because most agencies in the public sector really do have a mission – an understanding of their purpose, a set of values, and a way of putting them into practice. For example, it would be extraordinary, in a local authority education department, to find that people had no strong views about the value of education. There are a number of alternative philosophies which justify the delivery of education, and the officials might take a variety of approaches. The aims of educational services include:

- *liberal education*: the development of each individual intellectually and socially to that person's fullest potential.
- *socialisation*: education is a method of transmission of social norms and values.
- education as *handmaiden*[58]: the education system serves the industrial process and the economy by producing a trained workforce.
- *social change* (or 'social engineering'): the education system has been seen as a means of bringing about social change.

In the UK, the most important principles tend to be liberal education, inclusion and vocationalism – gearing education to the labour market. But education is a universal service, and people who work in it tend to have a belief in the importance of that in principle. The idea of a 'service ideology' is again relevant. People who work together work on similar policies, share views and perceptions, experience common constraints. The same kind of argument can be made about each of the public services. There are strong traditions: examples include the powerfully activist tradition of environmental health officers, the neo-liberal agenda associated with economic development, or, in housing management, the balance of the judgmental paternalism which reflects the influence of Octavia Hill[59] with the procedural correctness and concern with 'fairness' demanded by the public.

This is very different from the work of the private sector, where many 'business people' will say that there is not much difference between what they do and what people are doing in a business which produces a completely different type of product. Their skills are skills like 'management' and 'leadership', and the context in which they exercise those skills is not the central issue. In the public sector, by contrast, one of the key motivating factors is the belief that the work people are asked to do matters in its own right. Services do, then, have a sense of 'mission'; it is unfortunate that formal mission statements do so little to clarify it.

Case study: Community planning in Scotland

The material which follows comes from a review of the content of community plans in Scotland. Community planning partnerships are led by local authorities. I asked the 32 Scottish local authorities for copies of their community plans. Some responses were drawn from the Internet, others from printed copies, and at the time of the enquiry five local authorities had not completed the process, leaving 27 plans.

Most of the schemes had a combination of three main elements:

- a statement of vision;
- identification of principal themes; and
- some consideration of methods, or courses of action.

The content beyond that core is variable. It may include background information about the area; statements of principle; targets for evaluating outcomes; and action plans, which identify the partners responsible for action and the timetable for implementation. The absence of these factors in the community planning documents does not mean that they have not been taken into account – usually they are in other related documents – but rather that they have not been included within the community planning process.

The mission or 'vision'. The purpose of the community plans is usually stated in terms of a 'vision'. Some plans also add principles, either explicitly or in some cases implicitly (for example, by writing an extended statement on partnership or participation). Aberdeen Council, for example, identifies three main elements in its vision: people, the city environment and identity. Two other principles are identified: social inclusion and sustainability. Fife Council's 'vision' is a long list of attributes.

Our vision is of a Fife in 2010 that is ambitious, highly skilled, creative, caring and able to make and take advantage of opportunities. Ambitious not just to help each individual achieve what is best for him or her, but ambitious to improve our environment, health, services, products and infrastructure. Above all, our vision is of a Fife where quality of life is improving for everyone, and where inequalities between individuals and communities are narrowing.

A list like this does not point either to the relationships between the issues, or to priorities within them.

Themes. The apparent prominence of topics depends on the way in which they are presented. Most have some sense of hierarchy: because 'visions' or general principles come before operational aims, broad categories of aims (like sustainability, prosperity and social inclusion) tend to be put above others (like environmental improvement, training and urban regeneration). The hierarchy goes, then, from vision, to 'themes' or lesser visions, to aims. But it was not clear that the vision had much effect in shaping the selection of themes. Aberdeen listed 14 categories, identified as 'challenges'; this included themes such as cleanliness, involvement through voluntary action and 'leading the city'. The relationship between the challenges and the vision is vague.

The plans can be difficult to classify. Stirling, for example, identifies:
- 13 priority areas for development;
- three principles – social inclusion, sustainability and quality services;
- seven themes, three of which are the same as the three principles; and
- three working groups – health and well-being, development and community safety, and lifelong learning and citizenship.

Glossing over some ambiguities, the topics which are included by most local authorities are the economy (26 out of 27), health (22), the environment (21), education and lifelong learning (21), and community safety (20). Topics mentioned by smaller numbers of community plans are social inclusion (14), communities (10), citizenship and participation (7) and caring communities (5, with three more referring to 'health and care').

The statements of vision, principal themes and aims are intended to give an indication of local authorities' perception of their role, and their current priorities. Some of the topics may seem to be beyond argument, like motherhood and apple pie. Hardly anyone is against economic prosperity, for ill health, or for unsafe communities. Other ideas are more contentious. 'Lifelong learning' is at odds with the traditional local emphasis on childhood education;'communities' can be exclusive as well as inclusive; 'sustainability' can be used to oppose economic development. Even so, they are widely and uncritically accepted. There is an undercurrent in the themes of a changing understanding about the role of local government in Scotland. It is striking that many of the priorities which are identified do not seem to relate directly either to the work that local authorities have done most of historically – the provision of social services such as housing and social work, public services like arts, leisure and public amenities, and planning – or to the current spending priorities of local government. There is a danger that statements of priorities which have not been thought through may have unexpected consequences for policy in the future.

Community planning is not just a prescription for policy; it also has to be understood as a process. The test of whether it succeeds is not whether the plan works, but how it affects governance; it should make policy explicit, help people to identify service priorities, and bring people together to work in partnerships. These are the kinds of test applied by the team evaluating community planning for the Community Planning Task Force.[60] Some of the plans give evidence of 'joined-up' thinking. There are themes which clearly reflect the influence of partnerships, especially with health boards and the police. Some themes, including the environment and social inclusion, have been adopted partly because of their currency, but also because they offer opportunities for integrated perspectives from a range of different agencies. There are two main reservations to make. The first is that some of the stitching together of policies seems clumsy at times. Several plans give lists, and the role of particular services is not always clear. As this refers to the bulk of local government activity, it is an important deficiency. The other is that there is some evidence of a continuing 'silo' mentality. Several of the themes – including health, caring communities, economic development and education – fall clearly in the territory of existing agencies, and some of the minority themes seem to reflect strong departmental cultures.

Values

Policy documents often make explicit statements about values. Examples are statements about empowerment, social inclusion or promoting health. Values are usually intended, in the same way as a sense of 'mission', to guide an agency's actions. Describing something as a 'guide' carries the implication that it is unlikely to be paramount; it will be taken into account as one factor among others. Even when values are strongly emphasised, there is little room for absolutes: people might say, for example, that they put the needs of their clients above everything else, but every agency has to consider other issues – even if it is only where the money is coming from.

Values which are expressed as part of a policy are generally expressed positively: they represent what the policy is trying to achieve. Examples are health, welfare or social justice. Many of these are specific to particular types of agency or policy. In a democratic society, however, there are also some general principles which run across service boundaries. Democracies differ in character, but they share a common approach to institutional governance. The key elements include:

- principles of *beneficence* – public services are there to serve the public. Public services are supposed to do good – for example, to improve people's welfare, to improve their health, to protect the vulnerable, or to reduce disadvantage. Bryson recommends an 'ethical analysis' grid with explicit consideration of the relative seriousness of effects, the vulnerability (or potential damage) to people affected, the possibility of compensation and the compatibility with overall objectives.[61] His approach is extraordinarily prescriptive, but it has to be better to make these issues explicit than to take them as read.

- principles of *citizenship* – public services belong to the public. Many are based in concepts of right or entitlement. (The main exceptions are criminal justice and penal institutions, where people may be held to have forfeited rights; but even in these cases there is often a presumption that the user's interests must be safeguarded.)

- principles of *procedure*. It may seem odd to elevate procedure to the sphere of values, but procedure is fundamental to the way that public services operate in a democracy. No less than electoral restraints, democracies are founded on the rule of law. In every public service, without exception, there are institutional constraints – financial, administrative or legal – regulating the behaviour of agencies.

- principles of *accountability*. Accountability takes several forms. 'Democratic accountability' is usually interpreted in terms of the structure of authority: even if officials are not elected, decisions in the public sector are taken by people who can be held to account in an electoral process. This is a fairly weak form of accountability. 'Professional accountability' implies that people in public services guarantee levels of competence and quality of service, and can be held to account for failure by their peers.

'Administrative accountability' implies that officials will be accountable to others who have the responsibility to supervise their actions. 'Legal accountability' arises because, where people can make legal claims against an agency, agencies have to be prepared to explain their actions in relation to any individual case.

Many principles are negative, rather than positive; they do not say what people should do, but they do say what they should not do. Negative guidelines are just as important as positive ones – and possibly more important. When an agency describes itself as 'empowering people', we cannot be sure what they will do, but it should at least mean that locking clients in solitary confinement should not be on the agenda. (This is not an imaginary example: it is what happened in the use of 'pindown' in residential care for children during the 1990s, a disciplinary approach which depended on isolation, humiliation and confrontation.[62])

Negative principles are often implicit, rather than explicit. It is unusual for all values to be identified directly: many of them are default positions which only become relevant when they are breached. Policies should not need to say that they are done honestly, impartially and without thought of personal reward for the officials who implement them, but clearly, when this does not happen, it can be taken as a legitimate basis for criticism. It is not usually considered necessary for a local authority in the UK to declare itself to be opposed to nepotism or swearing at members of the public, because, even if they happen, they are relatively rare. Umberto Eco once commented that if you want to know what the problems of an agency are, look at their rules and assume the opposite.[63] This happens because the issues which people feel are important enough to make statements about are often those which are in doubt. For example, community care plans do not say much about managing fraud or physical abuse, not because they never happen, but because these are not the areas that planners feel they need to make statements about. The plans do, however, have a lot to say about treating people as individuals, giving them a voice and ensuring a joined-up service. When you read this, you can be certain that people are being made to fit into preconceived categories, that users' wishes are being overridden, and that all sorts of different services are coming in to deal with them at different points. Eco's rule may be a little cynical, but it is not wildly off-target.

In cases where the policy analyst identifies a contradiction between a policy and the stated values, the policy analyst's course of action is clear: the conflict should be reported back for consideration. Inconsistency between aims, or between stated principles and practice, is just the sort of thing that policy analysts are supposed to be identifying, and it needs to be reported if the policy is to be made effective. The other case, which is much more problematic, is where policies are deliberately unethical. This can overlap with illegality, but it is not the same thing. Illegality in the public sector is usually innocent – it takes the form of irregular procedure, rather than skullduggery – and policy makers will not usually want inadvertent illegality to be overlooked. Many ethical conflicts arise, by contrast, because the policy makers think the policy is justified regardless of other people's ethical objections (arguing, for example, that security takes priority over individual rights, or that the needs of local residents override equal opportunities), and a policy analyst's ethical reservations are not likely to be welcomed. Faced with a policy which is immoral –for example, a policy which is discriminatory, unjustifiably punitive or harmful – the policy analyst may need to argue for change. That, as I argued earlier, is a greatly constrained activity.

Aims

Aims are the starting point of policy, and the frame within which policy is set. What the policy was supposed to do is usually the main test for evaluating whether it has worked. Understanding aims is consequently basic to policy analysis. In the process of analysis, the establishment of aims provides the terms on which the analysis proceeds – an agenda for the analysis. Without that framework, there is no basis for focusing on particular issues, and the analyst would need to consider everything about the policy. This is also why, in a policy analysis, aims need to be considered lexically before the evaluation of the environment – a significant difference between policy analysis and policy formation.

A small example might help. At the time of writing, I am in the middle of an evaluation of an initiative concerned with community engagement and participation in housing developments. Without a prior statement of aims, the issues that would need to be addressed would be everything – consideration of communities, or housing issues, of approaches to community work, and so on. The agenda would be massive. But this is an analysis of a particular policy, and it is being done for a purpose. The aims of the initiative are:

1. the promotion of 'balanced and stable' communities;

2. the engagement and empowerment of communities, as an issue
   in its own right; and
3. the facilitation of development.

This is necessarily a narrow focus. Even within the scope of what
could be done about the policy itself, it is concentrated on particular
issues. The kinds of issue which are *not* part of the aims are: to generate
income; to educate or develop public awareness of issues; or to consider
how the initiative might be developed by other agencies.

These are issues which might conceivably be relevant – if the issues
came up, I would draw them to the attention of the commissioning
agency – but they are not part of the agenda for the analysis.

Aims have to be operationalised, or translated into practical terms.
If this has not been done before a policy analysis, it has to be done
during it. There has to be some way of deciding whether a policy has
worked, and it is not possible to make that judgment if there are no
criteria by which it can be done. Typical aims include:

- responding to problems – for example, providing health care, or
  improving slum housing;
- satisfying claims for services – for example, providing health care,
  or offering nursery provision;
- undertaking a desired activity – such as, mounting a celebration
  or founding a museum;
- improving outcomes – such as, more women finding
  employment, or better examination results for pupils.

This often gets shortened into a phrase like 'meeting needs': one of
the standard questions used by the Audit Commission is: 'is the service
meeting the needs of the community and/or users?'.[64] 'Needs' could
mean many different things – a problem, a range of responses, or a
claim for service – but the idea is a useful test of whether a response
can be said to be appropriate to the circumstances.

Michael Scriven is very critical of planning and management based
in aims, and although his main focus is on evaluation, which comes at
the end of the process of analysis, it seems appropriate to mention
some of those criticisms at this stage. The problems with working to
aims, in his view, include these:[65]

- that the process is biased in favour of the perspective of service
  management, against service users. If users have a different
  perspective, a tight focus on aims will not leave room for it. This
  is an important potential criticism. The main way to forestall it

is to ensure that the aims which are identified have been based, at the outset, in some degree of consultation or participation;

- that aims and goals need to change; they cannot be set once for all, but need to be interpreted flexibly, as policy develops;
- that the tests of good policy have to go beyond explicit aims, to other, unpredictable dimensions. One of his examples is the evaluation of consumer products: people are not just concerned with whether the product does what it is supposed to do, they also care about safety, reliability, and lots of other hidden and ill-defined issues that become important when they are breached. In this book, I have tried to anticipate this criticism by prior consideration of 'values', but it is fair to acknowledge that there may be negative, concealed aims – things which a policy was supposed not to do (such as costing the earth, generating embarrassing problems in the media, or antagonising users of alternative services) but which only become apparent when it has done them.

The process of identifying aims is not always straightforward. It can call for a process of negotiation and interpretation. Some policies are not really there to do what they say. Some agencies are happy to admit privately that work in deprived areas is concerned to bring employment into the area, rather than to do what the project said on the application for funding. Some policies, and some agencies, change tack – they start with one set of objectives, and find that they need to work to a different agenda. Some policies are negotiated compromises, made deliberately less likely to be effective as a way of balancing the claims of competing interest groups. Deliberate loopholes can be left in the rules, because without them the policy will not be agreed. Beyond that, although it may sound strange, it is not obvious that policy is intended to have any effect at all. Some policy is there because it has a symbolic importance. Governments feel it is important to be 'tough on crime', to support families, or to respect diversity. These kinds of policy are often associated with token gestures. And there are issues where the aim is not so much to have an effect as to do what is possible. No-one seriously believes that governments can save every child being neglected by parents, but governments have to do something, and there are a range of interventions, typically including maternity visiting, social work and child protection services. There are many failures, but failures are not the point: the point is that someone has to try.

In practice, aims are not necessarily adequately formed or workable. Sometimes the aims of policy are misconceived – like policies to intervene in the 'cycle of deprivation', when the evidence available on the dynamics of deprivation has found that the cycle of deprivation does not happen.[66] In some cases, aims prove to be impossible to achieve in practice. (For example, it has been the law in the UK for over 50 years that public housing providers have to give 'reasonable preference' to large families when they allocate housing. Because large families need large houses, they are hardly ever in competition with small families in practice. The law is a dead letter.) Sometimes the aims of policy are contradictory – like policies for equality which try simultaneously to equalise the position of groups with the rest of society, and to reduce disadvantage within those groups.

In a professional context, policy analysts can point to contradictions (or, more diplomatically, 'tensions') in a policy, but they are unlikely to have the liberty to say straight out that a policy was ill-conceived in the first place. Criticism of the aims can be phrased as an invitation to revise the aims of the policy in the light of the findings of the evaluation. There are, however, two particular circumstances where policy analysts may need to criticise the aims of policy directly, and make the case that the aims must be revised. The first is where the policy is unethical. The other is where the policy is illegal. Deliberately criminal action by public sector organisations is unusual in most developed countries; criminal behaviour is generally attributable to the actions of individual officers, rather than the decisions of the agency. By contrast, inadvertent or casual breaches of the law – especially breaches of statutory duty and rules relating to procedures – are commonplace. Typical examples are policies which have not caught up with a change in the law, or policies which attempt to favour one group – political constituents or local businesses – in ways which are incompatible with rules about discrimination. The policy analyst is not usually responsible for policy making, and consequently cannot bring about change, but there is a duty to report the illegality to the decision makers. The general advice for a policy analyst, and indeed for most people within an organisation, is to 'cover your back': public servants should not leave themselves open to the charge that they were aware of misdemeanours and did nothing, or worse, that they were complicit in them. External consultants need to make a formal statement in writing, in the first instance to the person within the organisation who they report to, and to keep a copy of all correspondence. The way to do this is not to seek to make an authoritative statement of the law; it is, rather, to raise the question as to whether the practice is in conformity with the requirements, and leave the decision to those in authority.

Goals

Aims and values have to be 'operationalised'. That means that they have to be translated into practical, or 'operational', terms, that can be acted on and tested. Setting goals or targets is a common way of doing this. The goal can be broadly stated, but if it is too broad, it is not really an operational criterion. Goals are often set in quantitative terms – for example, the UK government's commitment to halve child poverty by 2010. The advantage of quantitative tests is that it makes it possible to say clearly whether or not targets have been achieved.

It may seem strange that goals should be operationalised before methods have been chosen. The idea of specifying desired outcomes – 'management by objectives' – has been part of an important shift in the pattern of governance. The implication is that the goal might be achieved flexibly by a range of methods. The World Bank, for example, used to instruct client countries about the approaches they considered desirable, and often it specified institutional structures closely; it has moved to a different model of governance, suggesting that countries can work out for themselves how the goals can best be achieved. The same is true within the UK government. Aaron Wildavsky has been particularly critical of the approach, because it often fails to take into account the question of available resources. Management by objectives leads to more discussion of objectives, and more paperwork, at the expense of 'programmatic activity' – that is, of time doing the job. He argues that:

> the attempt to formalize procedures for choosing objectives without considering an organisation's dynamics leads to the opposite of the intended goal: bad management, irrational choice and ineffective decision making. It is not that sophisticated analysts do not realize the pitfalls but that, having dug the pits themselves by semantically separating objectives from resources, they are surprised when client organizations fall into them.[67]

The UK government's advice is that targets should be 'SMART':

- specific;
- measurable;

- achievable;
- relevant; and
- time-bounded.[68]

This sounds initially reasonable, but it should not be taken for granted. Vague targets can indicate the direction of movement without being too specific on how far one has to go; aiming, for example, to cut deaths from cancer, or to recruit as many people as possible from minority ethnic groups, does not need to have a fixed target. If a goal is very specific, it tends to imply not just that we know what the policy ought to achieve, but how it should be done. The idea that goals must be 'achievable' before they are set conceals assumptions about method and approach. If SMART targets are set, there is at least a risk they are being set in the wrong order.

Specific objectives are not only geared to results; they can be concerned with the process and management of a service. Ambrose, writing about urban regeneration, distinguishes three types of performance indicator. Some are concerned with *structure* – the organisation of services or programmes. Some are concerned with *process* – the way in which policy is put into practice. And some are concerned with *outcomes,* or the results of policy.[69]

There are many disadvantages in precise targets. Probably the best-known problem is that the targets take over policy, and that less tangible objectives are sacrificed in the determination to achieve the targets at all costs.[70] An example is the attempt to reduce lengthy waiting lists for hospital care. The policy to reduce waiting time has had many beneficial effects. But it has also changed service priorities: one reason why some people were waiting a very long time was that their condition was considered less urgent, or less dangerous, than some other conditions. Throughput – the number of cases treated – has been more important than the quality of service. Alcock comments on the same problem in another context: targets in area-based initiatives have tended to 'steer' the management of policy in the direction of inputs and outputs, rather than outcomes.[71]

A second problem has been manipulation of the figures. There have been controversies where service delivery or practice has been distorted in order to present the figures in the best possible light. The Commission for Health Improvement suggests that:

> One of the reasons for long delays in A&E [Accident & Emergency] departments accepting patients from waiting ambulances may be their own need to achieve a target that

no patient should wait more than four hours from arrival in A&E to admission, transfer or discharge. This illustrates how targets set for one service may act against cooperation between services.[72]

The third problem is too much is expected from the objectives. Long lists of targets, Wildavsky argues, become a way of providing excuses – 'mechanisms for avoiding rather than making choices'.[73] Agencies focus on the tasks they can achieve and jettison the ones they cannot. But, at the same time, 'everyone knows that the objectives of many public agencies are multiple, conflicting and vague'[74] – which means that short lists are unconvincing and inappropriate.

Fourth, the issue which is being dealt with might not be one which lends itself to operationalisation in terms of simple, practical targets – in which case planners may be tempted to substitute a more manageable, less 'wicked' problem. 'Indicators', Alcock comments, 'do not just become a proxy for real social change, they become a substitute for it'.[75] Poverty, for example, is a complex, multidimensional issue. 'The poor' are not a consistent, predictable group of people; many people are vulnerable to poverty, and many people experience the problems of poverty for limited periods of time. That means that decision makers cannot spend money on the problems of poverty and be confident that the problems they are dealing with will become smaller, that the numbers of people apparently in poverty will fall, or that the people who are being helped will be identifiable as poor in three years' time. Money for 'poverty' tends to be spent, at the local level, on 'communities' and redeveloping housing estates: the houses are easy to count, improvement is visible, and the houses cannot get up and walk away. The need to make goals achievable and politically acceptable can determine what sort of problem is likely to be addressed.

Case study: Performance indicators in the NHS

The NHS operationalises its targets in a lengthy series of 'performance indicators'. These are selected statistics used as signposts to show how the service is performing. Using this kind of target developed after the Griffiths report in 1983:[76] Roy Griffiths, a supermarket manager, was used to assessing the performance of Sainsbury's every morning through summary information, and was reputedly astonished that the NHS was unable to do the same.

NHS indicators are intended to be SMART. The indicators for health authorities cover six main areas:

- health improvement;
- fair access;
- effective delivery of appropriate health care;
- efficiency;
- patient/carer experience;
- health outcomes.[77]

The list of indicators is very long, and some would require detailed explanation. The short section on 'patient/carer experience' can help to give a feel of what the indicators are like. The indicators used in this section are:

- six-month inpatient waits;
- 13-week outpatient waits;
- two-week cancer waits;
- delayed discharges;
- access to a GP.

These indicators are based on figures which are easily available. They are all concerned with inputs, or what the service does; they are not concerned with how patients or carers feel about the service. They are not concerned with quality or with results. They do not refer to other issues in the experience of patients, like information, notice periods and reliability of treatment, which are controversial but are not among the tests. And they have been bitterly criticised for distorting service priorities – leading, for example, to accelerated treatment for low-priority cases, and to the elevation of waiting lists above clinical effectiveness.

The indicators for 'effective delivery of appropriate health care' have attracted less attention, and raise other issues. They include:

- breast cancer screening;
- cervical cancer screening;
- surgery rates for coronary heart disease;
- surgery rates for joint replacement;
- surgery rates for cataract removal;
- number of GPs;
- increase in the numbers of drug misusers accessing drug treatment services.

These are, again, input measures. Beyond the issue of delivery, they depend on some key assumptions about priorities. Screening for breast and cervical cancer is no guarantee of screening for other cancers, like bowel or prostate cancer. Surgical intervention is not a good indicator of the appropriateness of treatment. And the *increase* in the number of drug users accepting treatment is not a good indicator of whether the service is meeting need – there may be a larger increase where services have previously been underdeveloped.

The issues relating to indicators in principle are considered further in Chapter Six.

Exercise

Review performance indicators on a topic included in the library of local performance indicators at www.local-pi-library.gov.uk. Are they fit for purpose?

FIVE

Assessing the environment I: qualitative interpretation

The most basic part of making an assessment of the environment is to find out what is happening. Finding things out is generally treated, in academic writing, as a form of 'research'. Research is an essential component of policy analysis – although properly speaking, it is not one component, but rather a term that stands for a wide-ranging set of issues. Unfortunately, the idea of research is beset with stereotypes, and many people, in practice as well as in the academic world, will respond to the demand to 'do some research' by doing what they have been taught to do. Many researchers are schooled to use disciplinary approaches to research, doing things the way that economists, sociologists or psychologists do them. People who are not very sure about research often imagine that it is some sort of exercise featuring questionnaires, tick-boxes and computers. Policy research is not like that – or at least, it should not be like that, because the object is to find out what can be found. Policy research, Majchrzak argues, deals with problems that are complex and multidimensional. It focuses on the kinds of issue which a policy can affect, rather than those it can't. It is heavily influenced by the needs of users. And it is also, crucially, value-laden; it is a moral, and political, activity.[78]

The term 'methodology' refers to the rationale people give for different kinds of method. There are several widely used distinctions between different types of methodology. The first lies between *inductive* and *deductive* approaches. 'Inductive' approaches begin by collecting material and seeking to classify and organise it after it is collected. An example is 'grounded theory', which sorts material by putting it into categories and stopping when there is no material left to classify.[79] 'Deductive' approaches begin with a hypothesis or model, against which circumstances can be compared. Hypotheses are theoretical predictions, or reasoned guesses, about what might be found. This is the approach favoured by Pawson and Tilley in *Realistic evaluation*.[80] Pawson and Tilley are experienced researchers; they develop hypotheses through a process of negotiation and discussion, where ideas about policy are established through knowledge of the literature, previous experience and engagement with practitioners. But their work depends on taking a limited number of perspectives on tightly defined issues. Generating hypotheses has serious disadvantages. Social research commonly begins with a research problem – an issue which requires investigation. In policy analysis, by contrast, the first thing to find out is what the problems might be, and it can be dangerous to assume that we know and understand the problems before this has been done. Hypotheses depend on prior knowledge – on the assumption that we already know enough about the issue to disregard other factors. This puts the blinkers on; it closes minds; it encourages analysts to assume that they might know the answer before they start. Majchrzak suggests:

> hypothesis testing ... has little place in policy research. While such an approach fosters thoroughness in scientific exploration, the potential loss and misperception engendered by taking a singular perspective on a multidimensional problem is too great a risk and luxury for policy researchers.[81]

A second, key distinction lies between *intensive* and *extensive* research.[82] 'Intensive' research looks in depth at a problem or issue, examining the relations between different elements and the processes involved. Intensive research is concerned with questions like why and how something happens. 'Extensive' research is concerned with the context and relationships within which an issue occurs; it is concerned with the extent of problems and associations between problems and issues. The distinction between 'intensive' and 'extensive' research is particularly important for policy analysis, because it tries to relate the pattern of research done to the kind of problem which is being addressed. The appropriate approach depends on what kind of problem we are dealing with. Much of my own work has been intensive – examples referred to in this book include studies of the experiences of psychiatric patients, the problems of people in minority ethnic groups in a rural area, and what kind of problems might stop elderly people in hospital being referred to services which could help them better. But other problems have needed an extensive approach, like comparisons of poverty rates in different areas, or planning services for people with dementia in an area. The pattern of research should be the best option for the circumstances, not necessarily the one the analyst is most used to doing.

Third, there is a distinction between *qualitative* and *quantitative* methods. Qualitative methods are those which are concerned with interactive investigation of a topic, examining process and relationships; quantitative methods use measurement to identify and test trends.

Although these are methods, rather than rationales, there is a strong link between qualitative methods and inductive approaches, and conversely between quantitative methods and deductive approaches.

This book is not an introduction to social research, which is a much broader topic than the issues considered here, and this chapter has a more specific focus. It asks what ought to be considered when trying to find out what the issues are in a policy analysis, and what the skills and techniques are that are needed to do the task. In formal research terms, what needs to be done first is inductive. Finding things out begins by looking to see what is there, not supposing that something is there and proving or disproving it.

Checking existing sources

Literature reviews

Policy analysis is not a strictly academic exercise, and the purposes of literature reviews are different from academic reviews. A literature review in policy analysis is mainly used:

- to identify what is known about a subject. One of the essential purposes of reviewing literature is to avoid 'reinventing the wheel' – spending time and money on something which has already been thoroughly checked out elsewhere;
- to identify methods and approaches which might be useful for the analysis of the issues. The academic literature is often helpful in providing frameworks or structures for organising disparate material relating to a field in practice. By contrast with many academic literature reviews, however, there is no place for a survey of areas of academic interest, disciplinary development, or the broader context;
- to bring evidence to bear which may reinforce or question findings from the policy analysis. If the findings are similar to findings from other places, it may be taken as confirmation of the problems. (For example, in a study I worked on about community safety in one part of Scotland, several business owners from minority ethnic groups told us they were repeatedly getting their shop windows smashed.[83] That sounds like a local issue, but another report from another region had found the same thing.[84] The literature review raises the possibility that this might be a general problem, rather than a problem specific to the area.)

These are limited objectives, and it follows that the literature review may also be limited. Wallace et al raise the question of whether a comprehensive, 'systematic' literature review is really necessary. They point to two main problems with comprehensive trawls. From an academic point of view, they tend to be insufficiently selective. It is important to exercise some judgment about what should be included. From a practical point of view, they are time-consuming and expensive. More is not necessarily better.[85]

Looking at records

A second important way of finding out what is happening is looking at existing records. This is useful not just as a way to find out what is happening, but for all the other main stages of policy analysis — a statement of aims, identifying methods, implementation and evaluation. That is so generally true that it can be done pretty much automatically. Even if we know nothing about the situation, we always know the first things that we are looking for: information about each stage of the policy process. That makes the records a good place to start.

Important as reviewing the records can be, looking within them for material about the environment is often a matter of luck and accident. Agencies rarely collate background data while they are starting up, because when they are starting up, they do not have a pool of information to draw on, and putting it together is not usually the first thing on their minds. When they realise that they ought to have done so, because they need that information to establish what difference they have made, they often ask consultants to construct a back-story or 'baseline' for them in retrospect. The best information tends to be collated by well-established agencies, like local government or the health service, where the procedures are already in place, and new initiatives tend to grow out of older ones.

Stakeholders

One common way of finding out what problems are is to ask the people who know. Policy research tends to be based on *purposive* samples. People are selected not because they 'represent' the population randomly, but because they have something to say on a process. It is common to identify the 'stakeholders' in a process — decision makers, officers, service users and agencies engaged in related work would normally be taken into account. Discussing issues with the stakeholders is important just to be able to gather information. The people who know about an issue are often the people most closely engaged with it, and it is not possible to find out what the issues are without asking. But it also has a political dimension: the process of discussing issues with people serves to identify the interests of stakeholders, and makes it possible for their views to be taken into account.

A stakeholder is 'any group or individual who can affect or is affected by the achievement of the organization's objectives'.[86] That is a very broad definition – potentially too broad to be manageable. For practical purposes, stakeholders can be thought of in three main categories. The first category consists of organisations, officials or agencies who are engaged directly in policy making. These are often people with specialised knowledge. Beyond that, they are also likely to be people who may be able to take responsibility for action. In Chapter One I mentioned the 'Star Trek' model, where analysts beam down for their report and then disappear afterwards. Working as an external assessor or consultant, making recommendations is all very well, but someone has got to do something about them. People need to have some sense of engagement, or even ownership, in the report, or nothing is going to be done afterwards.

The second category of stakeholders includes people on the receiving end of policy – people who are directly affected by decisions. A decision to close a town's hospital, for example, affects the staff who work there; it affects people providing services in the vicinity, such as the local authority or voluntary organisations; it affects other services who rely on the hospital to do their own work, like GPs and community nurses; it affects patients, who may or may not be represented by patients' organisations; and it affects the general public, who even if they are not patients, may become so.

This broad category of stakeholders includes organisations and agencies as well as service users. Their role is often particularly important. Organisations, Catt and Murphy suggest, adopt three main positions in these processes. These are:

- information provision: organisations pull together data from a range of sources;
- 'contestation', or advocacy: organisations adopt positions in relation to policy questions;
- synthesis: bringing together different types of information, position and voices.[87]

These roles are enormously helpful for policy analysts; effectively, such organisations do part of the job that needs to be done, as a way of gaining leverage in the policy process. But the information and presentation is often partisan or selective, and some caution needs to be exercised.

A third category of stakeholder also needs to be considered: the citizen. In a democracy, there are arguments not just for enlarging the information base, but for the general involvement of members of a political community in decision making.[88] The concept of political 'participation' stretches from the rather limited engagement required in voting, through to active participation in deliberation and decision making. In its most complete form, the concept of participative democracy offers an alternative approach to the policy process, but that is not the purpose of considering it here. The nub of the argument is that the public are the source of political legitimacy, and so the public must be able to make the decisions. Every citizen, by definition, is a stakeholder. This is an argument for having public meetings, and making decisions in public forums. Participative concepts have been particularly influential in housing, planning and community regeneration. Increasingly, decision making proceeds by a slow process of engagement, discussion and deliberation in public.

Key actors

There is an overlap between the categories of 'stakeholders' and 'key actors', but they are not quite the same thing. A stakeholder is someone, or some organisation, who is affected by decisions, or who participates in them. That is a very general set of issues, and it can include large numbers of people. A key actor is someone who has an important role in the policy process – often someone whose position brings them into contact with a range of other actors. This is potentially a much more limited group of people.

There are two main ways of identifying the key actors. The easy way is to use some general model from the academic or management literature. One model I have found especially useful is David Billis's work in *Welfare bureaucracies*. Billis identifies five 'strata', or levels, of operational work. The five strata are:[89]

> 5. *Comprehensive field coverage.* This includes policy making and planning. Officers and decision makers at this level are presented with a range of needs, and have to identify appropriate services to meet them. Community planning, health improvement or transport strategy are conducted at this level.
> 4. *Comprehensive service provision.* This is the organisation and direction of a complete service, like a housing department, a

social services department, an education department or a hospital. The directors of these services have a general remit to deliver services in their area.

3. *Systematic service provision.* This is about the provision of parts of a service, dealing with a range of problems. A social services department will usually have a range of sub-divisions, such as area teams, social work with families, domiciliary social care, and so on. In a hospital, consultants are responsible for teams covering different wards and units, such as geriatric care, psychiatric care, radiology, and so on. These are all parts of a broader system.

2. *Dealing with problems as situations.* Professionals are presented with problems, and have to decide what to do about them. This kind of work is done by people in a wide range of activities – doctors, social workers, teachers, health visitors, area housing managers and police officers.

1. *Dealing with problems as demands.* People who work at this level have defined tasks, and usually there are rules or guidance on how they are supposed to deal with them. Receptionists or social security officers are examples.

This scheme is very different from a conventional 'organisation chart'. Organisation charts show the lines of formal accountability, and how teams are defined. Many are written from the top down, without necessarily giving a clear idea of what the relationships really are; others look like blueprints of the office heating system. Billis's classification, by contrast, helps to predict who is going to work on certain classes of problem, and who is going to come into contact with other people.

The other main approach is to identify the actors, and their relationship to each other, through a process of enquiry. Bryson suggests beginning with a small group of people in a workshop, and using them to identify relationships and connections, including an evaluation of the relative contribution, power and importance.[90] This has the advantage of speed, but it might prejudge the issues. Identifying relationships and interactions is typically done over a period of time, as information from each actor is collated with others.

The analysis of the relationships needs them to be mapped, or grouped together, in a way that makes it possible to see the relationship of each key actor to others. Usually this is done through a form of 'systems analysis'. Systems theory has become unpopular, partly because the books about it are stuffed with some appallingly impenetrable jargon, and partly because it has come to be associated with a 'functionalist' perspective in sociology, but it is a basic tool. (It should also not be confused with the idea of 'systems management', a top-down management model which is about something quite different.[91]) The idea of the 'system' is a way of thinking about any complex operation. Systems analysis is used, for example, to describe the workings of the human body, or servicing a car. So, the human body can be said to have a digestive system, a nervous system, a muscular system, and so on; while a car has a steering system, a braking system, an electrical system, and so forth. Systems theory points to two main issues. The first is that any complex system can be broken down into sub-systems, and each of those systems can be described separately. The second main point is that each of the sub-systems is interrelated. Describing complex issues in terms of 'systems' means that:

- the system needs to be broken down into its constituent parts;
- there has to be some description of the relationship between the parts; and
- some of the constituent elements can be described as systems in their own right.

This, more or less, is what to do to identify the role of key actors in a process. If the system is very simple, it will be enough to identify the role of each actor in relation to each other, and to the group. As it gets more complicated, it becomes necessary to identify sub-groups, and look at the way they interrelate.

An example may help to make this clear. Imagine, for example, that the process which needs to be analysed is the delivery of educational support for a child suffering from a hearing impairment. The basic 'systems' to be examined are:

a. the child and the child's family – the most important system to consider;
b. the school, including sub-systems like learning support;
c. the delivery of primary medical care; and
d. specialist support from hospital care, usually including diagnostic and treatment options.

There may also be other types of system depending on circumstances, such as voluntary organisations and supportive social networks. A systematic, purposive sample of key actors should include at least one respondent from each system.

Research methods: obtaining information

There is a vast literature on research methods, and I am not going to attempt to cover it here. For practical purposes, the basic techniques for drawing information from purposive samples, like stakeholders and key actors, are qualitative research techniques – individual interviews, group interviews and postal enquiries. When samples are selected for a purpose, such as finding out what relationships there are, any questions that are asked need to be compatible with that purpose. Unless samples have been selected with mathematical representativeness in mind, there is no point in questions which establish proportions or fixed answers. Questions to stakeholders and key actors generally need to be exploratory, giving respondents the chance to identify the issues that matter. That implies that they should give the respondents the chance to identify the issues that matter from their perspective. 'Open questions' are questions which cannot be answered with a single, fixed, response, like 'yes', 'no' or 'three years ago'. 'Closed' questions are questions which can be. Closed questions are not much use in this context; questions generally need to be open.

Individual interviews are the most used technique. An interview is a purposive conversation. It is a 'conversation' because there are two sides: the person being interviewed, generally with the aim of finding out information, and the person who is doing the interview, who is asking questions and trying to steer the conversation to salient points. It is possible to conduct an interview entirely with pre-set questions. This is called a 'structured interview'; its main purpose is to put similar points to a range of people, so that answers can be gained in a form which can be compared directly. Structured interviewing is mainly used in specialised forms of research, such as market research and opinion polling, where set answers make it possible to quantify the results. This is occasionally helpful for policy analysis, but it is not typical of the process, and it is not a central skill. What is much more often done is interviewing in depth. Interviews cannot be 'unstructured', because they must have a purpose; generally that means that there is an agenda, a list of topics which is to be covered, or some way of structuring the material that the interview covers. Interviews in depth are free-flowing. 'Semi-structured' interviews are a half-way process: interviewers have themes, and some initial questions, but are then free to examine issues in depth as they are raised. This is probably the most used technique for a team of analysts, because it makes sure that different people are asking the same things, while leaving analysts the freedom to go into more details when new issues arise.

Group interviews make it possible to identify shared perspectives, and points of disagreement. They are a quick and effective way of getting material from several people at once. In practical terms, they can be difficult to record. (Tape-recording in a group is difficult at best; when you visit an organisation or a community group it is hardly ever possible to choose the room where the group is taking place, or to control background noise while the interview is happening. Frankly, old-fashioned note-taking works better.) The main disadvantage with group interviews in principle is that people will feel some pressure to make their answers consistent with each other, which happens particularly when some people in the group have higher status than others. To avoid that situation, it is possible to give participants an individual questionnaire first. For larger groups, such as the public meetings used in stakeholder and user consultations, there are a range of techniques, including breaking people up into small groups and getting someone to record what people say on a flip chart, or using coloured sticky 'post-it' notes so that people can make comments on particular issues.

Postal enquiries deserve special consideration. They are fairly widely used in policy analysis, and that stands in striking contrast with most social science research. The problem for social scientists has been that postal enquiries are not much use for extensive, quantitative research, where they offer poor and unrepresentative response rates. This is not necessarily a limitation for qualitative work, however, and it hardly applies at all in work with a limited range of key actors or stakeholder groups, especially organisational representatives. If you want to find out, for example, the kinds of issue that patients' groups are taking up with local hospitals, or how housing associations go about managing empty property, writing to them makes perfectly good sense. I have used postal enquiries to some effect, mainly by keeping the size of the query down, using open rather than closed questions and focusing on drawing out information which was reasonably sure to be available. The main limitation of postal enquiries is that they do not give the same opportunity as an interview to explore issues which are unclear or which need further development. Where there are large numbers of potential stakeholders, however, they can be a very effective way of gathering information, giving people the opportunity to identify issues, and creating an opening for people to participate.

Case study: Referral processes for elderly people

This is an example of a simple postal enquiry used to draw information from a large number of stakeholders. The issue concerned referral processes for elderly people within the health service. It did not go to every stakeholder, or everyone affected; most obviously, it did not go to people who were being treated. A colleague and I circulated three questions to each main department covered by a local health authority:

1. Do you deal with elderly people who you feel would better be placed or treated elsewhere? If so, what are the circumstances?
2. Are there circumstances in which elderly people in your care could not be referred on or placed appropriately because options were limited or unavailable? What happens in such cases?
3. Are there other problems you see in the range of services available to elderly people?

It should be obvious immediately what this is not. First, it is not a numerically representative sample. This was a fishing expedition, attempting to identify what the issues were by giving professionals an opportunity to respond. Second, it is not a survey asking people to tick boxes. The questions are open and they invite respondents to expand on the issues of concern. We received a wide range of responses – 147 in all – of which about a quarter came from teams rather than individuals.[92]

The problems they described mainly referred to people who were mis-referred because of practical constraints, rather than any direct failures in the service. Here are some illustrative answers. Complaints about 'bed blocking', frequently reported in other surveys,[93] were not made everywhere, but there did seem to be recurrent problems:

> Many patients have to be admitted to acute medical beds because places are just not available quickly enough in residential homes for the elderly or long-term or respite.... The problems of the elderly would be minimised if the speed of transfer out of hospital could be maximised.... Patients remain in hospital with the danger that they will become more and more institutionalised.

Some respondents expressed concern about the limited availability of convalescent and long-term nursing facilities.

> As a high turnover unit we would benefit greatly from the provision of a fast reception service for elderly patients who have no continuing need to be on an acute urology ward but whose health or whose home circumstances make immediate discharge impossible.

There was also a suggestion that people were being referred for higher levels of support because other facilities were not available.

> Patients are often admitted to continuing care wards when they would have gone to a rehabilitation ward. They are sometimes transferred there when a bed becomes available.

These are short answers, and a more detailed, more expensive study would have identified and investigated the issues in more detail. What the postal enquiry did was to pool information, quickly and cheaply, from a range of actors with expert insight into the problems. It drew up an initial map of flashpoints and problem areas, identified a series of problems in administrative procedures, laid out an initial agenda for consideration, and provided a series of issues for further investigation.

Consultation

Consultation uses many of the same techniques as research, but it is not directly equivalent. It serves many purposes, and here are a few of them.

- *Democratic participation.* Democracy is often interpreted as meaning that people are responsible for their own government. In most of the western world, this is taken to mean representative government, a system of government based on accountability. But there is another strong tradition which sees democracy in terms of popular participation in decision making. Inviting people to contribute to decision-making processes is part of a broader commitment to political participation.
- *Deliberative democracy.* Another school in democratic thought identifies democracy with approaches to governance, such as negotiation and discussion, the representation of interests or the legitimisation of dissent. Joshua Cohen argues for a model of 'deliberative' democracy which emphasises democracy's character of discussion, cooperation, equality and social inclusion.[94] Consultation about policy fits squarely with this model.
- *Voice.* The idea of 'voice' originally came not from politics, but from thinking about economics, in an attempt to capture what kind of factors affected consumer behaviour besides price. People need to have some mechanism short of 'exit', or getting out of a process, to be able to register their views and opinions. This is

done in lots of ways – for example, through making complaints. Consultations have seized on the idea of 'voice' as being part of the function of a consultation. At the level of the individual, giving each person an opportunity to contribute allows that person to raise issues that matter, to have a sense of participating, and to have some sense of a stake in the process. At the level of groups, people exercising voice should also feel some level of empowerment and the ability to affect the outcomes of the process.

- *Alternative perspectives.* One of the simplest arguments for consultation is that it makes it possible for people to express different, or contradictory, opinions from others. The people who respond to consultations, for whatever reason, have a range of points of view. Some of them – even one of them – may just be right.
- *Legitimation.* Public agencies which consult generally claim that the consultation makes their final decision more legitimate. Usually they will find some way of establishing that their view has been supported. But they are not wrong to make the claim: other things being equal, a process which has been subject to consultation is more legitimate than one which has not been.

The test of a consultation is not that the balance of views represents the population as a whole. Usually, it will not: responses will be confined to those with an interest. Rather, what matters is that people have had the opportunity to respond, and that a diverse range of opinions has been gathered. A recent consultation on public marches in Glasgow received about 3,600 responses, of which over 3,400 came from members of the Orange order.[95] If this was supposed to be 'representative' of the population in a statistical sense, it would be a massive failure. But the numbers are not what matters. Much more important is whether the full range of views was included – and so, whether the last 200 expressed different views. None of the objectives of consultation considered here implies that a consultation has to be representative of the population. It may be a matter of concern if a consultation was exclusive – cutting out views which were inconvenient or against the wishes of decision makers. But it would equally be a matter of concern if the valid concerns of individuals or small minorities were overridden because a consultation represented the population in a statistical sense.

Case study: Designing schools

This is an outline of a consultation on the design of schools, which I undertook for a Scottish local authority.[96] The object of the consultation was:

- to obtain a wide range of views about the circumstances, needs and priorities for the physical development of schools;
- to engage stakeholders in the process of decision making; and
- to give stakeholders the opportunity to define agendas for action.

A questionnaire was used to obtain comments from stakeholders, including teachers, support staff, officials, community organisations, elected representatives and parents. 538 people responded. About half the responses came from teachers and head teachers: the remaining half came from a diverse range of other people with an interest in schooling. 131 pupils were consulted in seminars, and they sent back further returns from school councils.

The questionnaire was confined to one side of paper, and asked open, qualitative questions. There were seven questions:

1. *Your role.* What is your role or interest in [the local authority's] schools?
2. *Teaching and learning.* What physical changes in schools could improve learning and responsiveness to pupil's needs?
3. *Social areas* (eg common rooms, dining rooms, theatres and assembly halls). How might rethinking these areas enhance the experience of pupils and other users?
4. *External facilities* (eg playgrounds, sports fields and car parks). What role do they have in a modern school?
5. *New community schools* use schools to offer a range of services delivered by multidisciplinary teams. What are the advantages and disadvantages of this approach?
6. *Security and access.* How can we balance the requirement for security with community access?
7. *Community.* How can we engage families and communities better in schools?

The purpose of the questionnaire was to draw out a range of comments from diverse people, not to determine the pattern of the answers. The final report is not, in consequence, organised in the same structure as the questionnaire. Comments were classified thematically – that is, by bringing related points together in one place. (This is sometimes called 'open coding'.) Where, for example, someone commented on two issues in response to a single section, the comment was split between different classifications. Many respondents listed their concerns; those lists were broken up and the topics presented in the relevant sections. The test of whether this type of questionnaire works is the extent to which it succeeds in identifying the concerns and issues affecting the people involved.

Much of this was presented, in the report, in the words of the people who made the comments. There was no attempt to count the number of responses. It is not appropriate to judge responses in terms of the number of times they appear: the respondents are not part of a numerically representative sample. When comments recur from a range of sources, they can be taken as cross-confirmation: despite the diversity of the sample, there was a firm general consensus on such issues as the need for increased space in schools, car parking and improved ventilation. Some issues, like acoustics or the need for distinct physical education facilities, were only raised by a few respondents, but there was still a clear cross-confirmation of problems. It is still possible that isolated respondents may raise points of importance. Examples in the report were a comment from a community organisation about meeting the regulations applying to community venues, a cook concerned about vehicular access to the kitchens, and a senior fire officer concerned with arson in schools.

The responses were very varied. Many respondents expressed concern about the state of local schools and asked for modernisation, repair and redecoration. The physical environment of many schools is perceived as dark, drab, dirty and dated. There was widespread demand for more generous standards of space and provision of rooms. Respondents asked for bigger classrooms, more classrooms, more social rooms, wider corridors, more individual space, more social space and more storage. Schools need offices, assembly halls, meeting rooms, practice rooms, gyms, and so on. There was almost universal dislike of open-plan schools, and considerable reservations were expressed about multi-purpose areas. There were many requests to upgrade facilities and equipment, including information and communication technology, furnishings, display facilities and drinking water. There was widespread and strongly expressed general support for the provision of car parking, play areas and sports fields, with very little disagreement. School security was the main issue on which opinion was divided. Most respondents saw security as more important than community access, or even paramount; a minority, however, felt that security measures were excessive, intrusive and likely to be ineffective.

Interpreting and processing qualitative data

If the tasks described here are done well, the data they reveal will be a jumble. (I mean this metaphorically, but if you are working with flip-charts and post-it notes, they may also be a mess physically.) The more thoroughly views and voices are identified and recorded, the more material there will be. There is an argument to say that it would save time and effort not to record more information than is absolutely needed, but there are strong arguments against this. Some of those arguments are practical. It is often not possible to know, at the outset, just which information matters and which does not. It is much more difficult to fill in gaps later than it is to leave out information that does not fit. But there are also arguments in principle for gathering lots of open-ended information. The things that people raise tend to be the matters that are important to them. Disregarding them is not the way to persuade people that the analysis is legitimate or soundly based.

The standard technique for collating material of this sort often goes under the grandiose name of 'grounded theory'.[97] Properly speaking, however, grounded theory is a developed technique for using material to generate theories iteratively as data is collected. The main technique used within it is 'open coding', and it is that technique I want to explain. Open coding works by looking for themes and issues within the material. Issues, comments and findings are grouped together thematically. From the material, some general issues emerge. When themes get to be too full of information, they can usually be split up into sub-themes. Where there is material that does not fit an existing theme, it can be put into a new category. The process carries on until all the material is grouped with other material.

This may make more sense with an example. The quotes in box 5.1 come from a small qualitative survey of councillors in Scotland, which I did with my colleague Ross Martin.[98] Forty-four councillors responded to the enquiry.

Box 5.1: Organising quotes thematically

- The role of local authorities
  - *Local authorities are being downgraded*
    'Gets worse – too many functions and powers being removed.'
    'Less money, bidding for three-year posts, Public-Private Partnerships and the Private Finance Initiative, House Stock transfer, council jobs done by private companies: the role of a councillor is diminishing fast.'
  - *There are increased duties*
    'More responsibility with less power to change things and to raise resources.'
    'We are now very much at the sharp end of service delivery, but no longer in control.'
  - *Financial constraints*
    'Money is so tight that the council is barely covering the statutory duties, never mind an expansion of service.'
    'Since reorganisation in 1995, have been forced into a never-ending cycle of imposing cuts in services.'
- Relations with central government
  - *Central government is restricting local government*
    'The pressure of central government control has restricted the role of councillors.'
    'Central government diktat.'
  - *The Scottish Parliament has reduced the role of local government*
    'Devolution applies from Holyrood as well as to it.'
    'The Scottish Parliament has diminished the role of local government.'
  - *The Scottish Executive holds local government in low esteem*
    'Parity of esteem which was offered has not been forthcoming. Decisions made without consultation by Scottish Executive.'
    'The eradication of decision making and the main perpetrator is the Scottish Executive.'
  - *Local government should be recognised as a legitimate, democratic authority*
    'Mutual trust and respect, derived from recognising the importance of our respective roles and in particular the relationship with the electorate'.
    'Partnership of equals. Local government is elected and accountable as Parliament.'
- The position of councillors
  - *Exclusion from decisions*
    'As a non-administration councillor, I have little role other than as a watchdog for my constituents.'
    'Lack of meaningful consultation.'
  - *Poor terms of service*
    'Local government doesn't enable you to survive – and when you leave you get nothing.'
    'Salary and allowance constraints: we need the pay and security to do the job full time.'

The grouping of comments and the identification of themes are open to interpretation. The purpose of sifting and sorting material like this is not to pass judgment, although sometimes judgments are implicit in the classification; it is to collate the information so that it can be presented effectively. The classification of topics and themes gives readers a way of coming to terms with the information and making sense of it.

Validation

There is sometimes, among practitioners, scepticism about the validity of the kind of material produced by qualitative enquiries. 'Validity' is concerned with the question of whether the material shows what it is claimed to show. Comments from individuals, and even from specialist experts, are likely to be dismissed as 'anecdotal'. By contrast, when they are presented as numbers, they are treated as 'facts'. There is an obvious temptation in policy making to play the game, and to present the material as if the numbers really did mean more than the comments. But the distinction is fairly nonsensical. The worth of opinions and comments does not increase because a number has been stuck on them; if anything, the process of turning comments and views into something that can be counted can act to distort the source material. The comments that people make in their own words are just as likely, and arguably more likely, to reflect their true views, perceptions and experience.

Qualitative material is usually verified in three ways. The first is the validity of the source. Research with stakeholders and key actors is often based on the principle that these are the people who know about the issues. Second, there is external cross-confirmation. The things people say may reflect experience elsewhere. Independent research reports, press reports of problems, or specialist literature may show that a problem is general, rather than specific to a particular study. Third, there is internal cross-confirmation. If several people say the same thing, that is usually evidence either of a common perception or a common experience. People sometimes confirm each other's statements because they do not like to contradict or argue; if they say it in different places at different times, the cross-confirmation is stronger and clearer. In the responses of councillors, in the previous section, I gave two quotes in each category, to emphasise that the comments were not from isolated individuals.

The best research usually uses a range of approaches, because this is the way to 'triangulate' or cross-validate the information. Triangulation works, in qualitative research, by identifying common themes, and looking for material that is confirmed by different people in different ways. Pawson and Tilley are critical of this kind of approach; they complain that there is no obvious way to weight the information, and that there is no basis to establish priorities between competing and conflicting accounts.[99] From the perspective of policy analysis, this is not much of a problem. This process is meant to assess the environment, not to arrive at the 'right' answer. The purpose is to identify information, to synthesise it, to make it accessible and manageable. Decisions about priorities are made at a much later stage, and they are not usually made by the policy analysts.

The main problem is knowing what to reject. Where information has been cross-validated, there is a good reason to include it, but it is not safe to assume either that apparently cross-validated material is true (390,000 people in the UK gave their religion in the Census as 'Jedi'[100]) or that anything which is not cross-validated can be left out. Sometimes only one person, in a key role, has a clear understanding of the issues. Sometimes a single example or complaint, a 'critical incident', can give some insight into a whole process. Sometimes one person in isolation might just be right. The usual way to report isolated information is to note that it is isolated, and leave the decision about its importance to the people receiving the report. They may find that the issue reflects their own experience; they may feel the issue merits further investigation; they may decide not to do anything. At least they will have been warned.

Exercise

Review a consultation report from www.odpm.gov.uk or www.scotland.gov.uk

SIX

Assessing the environment 2: quantitative interpretation

Indicators

Extensive research attempts to consider the extent of an issue – how big it is, and what proportions are involved. This is usually a quantitative exercise. Quantitative data are used at many points in policy analysis. They tend to give the impression of accuracy and precision, and it is probably appropriate to begin with a health warning. The kinds of problems which are dealt with in public policy are often fairly ill-defined, and the implications are often uncertain. Numbers are used to give shape to issues, and to identify relationships. This is generally interpreted, in policy studies, as work on 'indicators'. An indicator is a statistic which is taken to mean something else besides the core information it contains.[101] It is a signpost.

The term 'indicator' is generally used to show that quantitative information about social issues represents not simple 'facts' but rather ways of putting together complex and uncertain information. The moment something can be counted, it is likely to be treated as if it was a 'fact'. Examples are classifications about whether a crime has been committed, or whether someone is unemployed. These are judgments, and they are open to argument. Indicators point out the direction, rather than showing 'the facts': they have to be interpreted.

Indicators are not the same thing as measurements. A good measurement is accurate, precise, and reflects the characteristics of the issue it is measuring. A good indicator is associated with the issue, robust, consistent over time and available. For example, low birthweight is usually a good indicator of poverty. It is a useful signpost to problems. Where there are large numbers of children being born underweight, we can be reasonably sure that people are poorer; where there are small numbers, people are probably richer. But low birthweight is not the same thing as poverty. At the individual level, we cannot tell how rich or poor someone is from the weight of their baby. Birthweight is a signpost, not a measure. Conversely, something can be a good measurement but a bad indicator. The measurement of criminal convictions is more accurate than recorded crime, and recorded crime is more accurate than crime surveys, but crime surveys are generally a much better indicator of what is happening than recorded crime or conviction rates.

Presenting indicators

There are three main ways of presenting indicators. The first is to use a 'headline' indicator: a simple, selective view. A good headline indicator is widely available, and easily understood. Commonly used examples are the use of income inequality as an indicator for poverty, or the growth rate as a proxy for economic development. These indicators are likely to be chosen because they are easily available and quantifiable, in preference to others which may be difficult or expensive to collect. In developing countries, infant mortality is widely used as an indicator of welfare: it is strongly linked with other issues, like poverty and adult health, and trying to improve it is a worthwhile exercise in its own right. The main problem with focusing on a headline indicator is that sometimes the indicator takes over the political debate − like the claimant count has for unemployment, or income levels for poverty. Complex issues need complex responses.

The second is to use a bank of multiple indicators − presenting long lists of indicators classified by theme. This approach is used in an annual report on deprivation, *Opportunity for all*[102]− more details are given in the case study on indicators of child poverty in this chapter. Hoernig and Seasons criticise conventional social, economic and environmental indicators in urban planning, because they are discrete and confined to particular issues.[103] That is only half right. Indicators are signposts, and single indicators can be interpreted in many ways. Indicators have to be interpreted; it is essential to 'read across' a bank of indicators, looking for trends. Social, economic and environmental indicators have to be read together as well as separately. If indicators are concerned with complex problems, multiple indicators help to 'triangulate' or examine a problem from different perspectives. Indicators which move in different directions can confuse, but they also point to contradictory trends; indicators which move in the same direction confirm general trends.

The third approach is to use a summary index. An example is the Index of Multiple Deprivation used in the UK to compare poverty by area,[104] or the Human Development Index used by the United Nations.[105] An index consists of a set of indicators which are compiled in order to produce a composite measure. The main issues are these:

- *Validity* – indices have to measure what they are supposed to measure, and cross-validation is difficult.
- *Reliability* – indices which are reliable within a particular social context, or at a certain period, are not necessarily transferable to other circumstances. The Office of Population Censuses and Surveys (OPCS) reports on disability seemed to offer excellent measurements of disability, but when the surveys were repeated, the apparent number of disabled adults had increased by over two million people in less than 10 years.[106] This is a very unreliable set of indicators.
- *Quantification* – the construction of indices tends to presume linear mathematical relationships. As I commented before, just because something looks like a number does not mean it should be treated like one.
- *Inclusion and exclusion of relevant factors* – exclusions lead to important issues being ignored. Over-inclusion can lead to excessive weight being given to particular factors; the high level of overlap in social phenomena related to deprivation makes statistical analysis difficult.
- *Weighting* – factors have to be given appropriate weights, which depends on appropriate quantification.[107]

In order to construct a composite measure, the numbers have to be standardised – they have to be the same kind of numbers (for example, proportions), describing the same kinds of thing. Common methods are the use of percentages or proportions; indices of urban deprivation have been based on Z scores, which are based on the relative position of a proportion within the overall distribution.

The issue of quantification is possibly the most pernicious problem. People get hypnotised by numbers. The moment that numbers are used, people assume they behave like numbers should – they can be added together, divided, proportions can be established, and so on. Social problems are neither ordinal nor aggregative. For example, figures for mortality cannot meaningfully be added together with figures for income to construct indices of deprivation – but we do this kind of thing all the time. Numbers are ordinal – two is greater than one – and aggregative – two plus two is four. Housing is not self-evidently more or less important than education, and a person with three problems is not necessarily worse off than someone with one. In the OPCS studies of disability, the points scheme used to measure disability was disregarded after the largest three problems were entered;[108] the experts who validated it felt, probably rightly, that after the three largest problems were taken into account, any others had only marginal weight.

It is possible to fix weights on issues normatively, in a 'points scheme': more points are given for the factors which people think are more important, but this runs the risk of being arbitrary. Several indices have been put together using multivariate analysis, which assigns values according to mathematical formulae. An example is the Jarman index,[109] which is used in the health service to pay GPs for certain social factors affecting the workload in their practices. Another is the Index of Multiple Deprivation, which is used to identify poor areas, and has a critical influence on funding for urban policy.

In theory, what is happening here is more than a mathematical calculation. It depends on a set of assumptions about the relationships between the data that are being linked. The Index of Multiple Deprivation identifies a range of 'domains' where deprivation occurs – for example, in the assessment of health and disability, crime, and education and skills for children and young people. The mathematical treatment is based on the central assumption that there is a central, underlying problem – more or less, the problem of poor areas – and that the different indicators are providing a range of perspectives on the core issue. The Oxford team who devised the Index of Multiple Deprivation explain the rationale as follows:

> It is hypothesised that an underlying factor exists ... that makes these different states likely to exist together in a local area. This underlying factor cannot be measured directly but can be identified through its effect on individuals.... These variables need to be combined at an ecological level to create an area score. Fundamentally this score should measure, as accurately as possible, the underlying factor.... The premise ... is that the underlying factor is imperfectly measured by each of the variables in the dataset but that the variables that are most highly correlated with the underlying factor will also be highly correlated with the other variables.[110]

Multivariate analysis is complex. The values assigned are generally decided by running the material through the computer, and they are difficult to argue with without specialised knowledge. You do not need to learn how to do a multivariate analysis, but if you are faced with one in practice you do need at least to know what the main criticisms are. The first problem is that the maths depend on certain assumptions about the data. As Noble and his colleagues recognise, the kinds of figures they are dealing with come from different sources, they are not strictly comparable, and they have different distributions.[111] For the maths to work, data are supposed to be normally distributed – that is, to reflect the distribution of a normal curve, and relationships are supposed to be linear – describable by a line on a graph. Despite what we read in statistics books, I have never encountered any social data in real life which were normally distributed. They all have to be 'transformed' and cut to fit the assumptions. Exceptional cases, or 'outliers', get thrown out of the analysis. Some data, like income distribution, can be made to fit the assumptions after transformation. But in other issues, like indicators of deprivation, the figures stubbornly refuse to look remotely normal even after all the standard transformations have been applied. To make up the Index of Multiple Deprivation, Noble and his colleagues followed up a range of transformations with 'shrinkage' of area data, adjusting data to reduce the effect of different sizes of area on apparent proportions. The results by the end of the process are still not quite normal, and not quite linear, but by the end of the process the team did not think that the discrepancies mattered very much.[112]

The second criticism is that the variables are supposed to be independent of each other (which sits uncomfortably with the idea that they are linked to some underlying factor). Unfortunately, in practice they are usually interdependent and it is difficult to distinguish effects. The computer will normally begin with the strongest relationship and weed out others which seem not to make a difference. When there is this sort of overlap – 'multicollinearity' – it matters crucially which factor goes into the analysis first.

The third problem is that the relationships are described in terms of associations, and associations change. The construction of the equation is built on a particular relationship, at a particular point in time. The Jarman index was based in research in the 1980s. Jarman sought responses from GPs about workload from their practices and processed the material after normalising data and attributing weights to different issues. But the workloads of GPs have changed, and there are new factors which might need to be taken into account – such as the workload created by people using illegal drugs.

Fourth, hardly anybody understands what on earth is going on in these formulae. This is sometimes seen as an advantage – a 'technological fix' to silence political opposition – but it is not necessarily helpful. Remember that you do not have to be a carpenter to know that a table wobbles.

Case study: Indicators of child poverty

The report *Opportunity for all*[113] uses a wide range of different indicators to give a sense of various dimensions of child poverty. Twenty different indicators are used to point to four key areas:
- improving family incomes;
- early years and education;
- quality of life; and
- transition to adult life.

The absence of a single, headline indicator makes it difficult to say with confidence that children have ceased to be in poverty, and this makes it difficult to say whether the government is succeeding in its target of ending child poverty by 2010. The Department for Work and Pension's (DWP's) consultation paper on child poverty consequently proposed four alternative approaches to providing 'headline measures' of poverty. The options were:
- 'a small number of multi-dimensional headline indicators';
- an index of a small number of indicators;
- a measure of 'consistent poverty'; and
- a core set of indicators of low income and consistent poverty.[114]

These options have the common problems of all summary indices. Summary indices lump together a range of issues, like income, health and social exclusion. Relatively 'minor' issues contained in *Opportunity for all*, like serious unintentional injuries, exclusion from school or teenage parents in education, would disappear from the analysis, because they cannot be allowed to distort the overall picture. Some values and weights would be difficult to spot, like the limited weight given to housing. And any of the options is vulnerable to influence of the size, number and association of problems.

When the DWP put this out to consultation, it was surprised by the support for multidimensional indicators, of the sort used in *Opportunity for all*. The problem is that indicators are used by a wide range of agencies, for many different purposes. Voluntary agencies are commonly asked by funders to identify the needs they are responding to, and to specify targets that are appropriate to their aims. The more detailed the indicators are, the better placed these agencies are to pick the indicators that are most relevant to their activity. The most useful indicators, then, are indicators that are capable of disaggregation at different levels – the more detailed, the better.

Enumerations and censuses

Enumerations are attempts to count things; censuses are attempts to count people. At local level, the most common form of enumeration comes from counts made of service statistics – the numbers of crimes reported or the numbers of people using particular services. These counts are subject to distortion, in two ways. The first is that, because they are based in service responses, any biases or omissions in the coverage of the services is carried forward to the statistics. For example, the system of assessment used for community care begins with individual assessments, which are aggregated to give information for purchasing services. If a service wants to know, for example, how many elderly people there are who need residential care, it can be done by assessing every old person and establishing how their position can be responded to. The fundamental problem with this approach, from the perspective of planning, is that individual assessments are conditioned by the range of services which is realistically available.

The second distortion is one which applies to all forms of census; some people are hard to find, or do not want to cooperate. This does not happen randomly – for example, young males cooperate less with censuses, and poorer people tend to be more mobile. This leads to systematic biases. The most problematic case of this is the census of population. This census is fundamental, because it provides the basis for most surveys and planning estimates. A census of population provides, in principle, a useful basis for the construction of indicators about a population, although a fluctuating population means, of necessity, that results can never be precise. It defines the denominators – the figures which are used to divide other figures and provide a proportion. The principal enumeration of the population in the UK is undertaken in the 10-year census. The main problem with the 10-year census is that it rusts: the data become gradually less and less reliable over time, to the point where the figures can be seriously misleading. Census data are between 2 and 12 years out of date at any point in time. The potential for social change within small areas is considerable, because of migration and redevelopment, and as a result the census is not very reliable as a basis on which to assess policy for small areas.

Statisticians have come to think that sample surveys may be better than censuses in assessing situations overall. This is because a well-constructed sample can avoid some of the systematic biases which are found in censuses. In France, the national census has been replaced with a rolling survey of the population, which offers a more secure basis for updating census material in the interim between counts.

Need assessment

The idea of 'need' is value-laden, and profoundly ambiguous. For some, it seems to mean little more than a problem – the numbers of people with disabilities, dementia or low financial resources can be presented as indicators of 'need'. For others, needs are demands for services: there are 'needs' for residential care, for home helps, and so forth. Properly speaking, a need is neither of these. On one hand, needs have to be needs for something; if people have a problem, but there is no service, it is not clear what the need is. On the other hand, needs are not just demands for particular types of service: there is no clear constellation of problems which identifies someone as 'needing' residential care, nursing care or the like. These are responses, and there are many possible responses to similar sorts of problems. Needs depend on a relationship between problems, on one hand, and the range of potential responses on the other.

There are many ways of establishing need. Bradshaw identifies four key concepts:

- *normative need*, which is need identified by experts. An example is the US poverty line, which is based on a measure of necessary expenditure on food.
- *comparative need*, which is need determined by comparison with others. People can be held to be in need if, for example, another area has a greater provision of services.
- *expressed need* is the need which people say they have. This is often identified with demand, but it is not the same as demand in economics, because it is not related to costs. Some people do not express demand because they think there is no chance it will be met; some will express demands strongly because, in the public sector, strong expression is often seen as the only way to get more basic services.
- *felt need* is the need that people feel, which may or may not be expressed. There are persistent problems of non-take-up of services, through ignorance, fear, and a sense of stigma.[115]

The establishment of priorities depends on other considerations than needs alone. In some circumstances (such as benefit receipt or community care planning) planning is based on the aggregation of individual assessments to yield a total figure, rather than an estimate of the overall size of the problem. Because services often fail to reach a proportion of the population served, it is inherent in such assessments that they are likely to understate the overall pattern of need in a community. Bradshaw's classification argues that some needs may be recognised, but not expressed. This poses a dilemma for planners: to what extent should provision be made for latent demand? The position is complicated by the processes through which demand is expressed: the demand often comes through referral by professionals after a non-specific request for service, so that the availability of particular options creates a channel or pattern of response to problems. To that extent, supply creates its own demand; and 'latent' demand is liable to become actual once services become available.

Needs assessments have become an important part of the assessment of policy. The shape of such policies is, roughly, that after an identification of needs, a range of appropriate responses is selected, and the test of whether policy is effective is whether the needs are met. There are various permutations of this formula, but it is used in a wide range of services: examples are medical services, services for elderly people, special educational programmes, anti-poverty strategy, social security provision, and housing provision. The dominant model of needs assessment in health and social care has developed around the idea of a census of needs – a comprehensive enumeration. The stages are:

1. The needs of every individual are assessed.
2. The figures are aggregated to produce a global result.
3. Services are commissioned on the basis of the global figures.
4. Services are allocated to individuals on the basis of their assessment.

This approach is beset with problems, and it makes very little sense in practice. If the aim is to respond to the needs of a population, assessing the individual needs of everyone in that population is not the best way to do it. From the point of view of the people planning and commissioning the services, assessing the needs of every individual is slow, expensive and unreliable – censuses miss people out, they have systemic biases, and by the time the census is done, needs will have changed. From the point of view of individuals in need, a global assessment does not help to deliver a sensitive, individuated response. If services are allocated immediately consequent to assessment, then stages (2) and (3) are redundant – they add nothing to the quality of the response, and they hold up the allocation. If they are not allocated immediately, the implied delay breaks the link between individual assessment and provision. People's needs change over time, and by the time the services are commissioned and delivered, the individual who has been assessed is not likely to be the person who benefits.

Needs assessments have to serve two purposes. In the first place, they are used to deliver services to individuals. Second, they have to be capable of aggregation in order to yield global figures. The first function implies diversity, individual responsiveness and complexity; the second calls for uniformity, simplicity and mechanisms to share information. No system of needs assessment has ever squared the circle. For policy purposes, there is a good argument for uncoupling the two different approaches. Planners need only the global figures, and it is not crucial if they are accurate at the individual level. For service delivery, the converse is true; global figures are not very useful if the range of people identified is not actually being served.

Forecasting

If measurement is a suspect activity, the measurement of the future – forecasting – is even more suspect. Forecasting methods are widely used for basic service projects. Every housing plan has to have some basic statement of present and future needs. To build a primary school, an education department has to make some kind of statement of what the population aged five to 11 will be in three years from the time of the decision, and then make decisions for the next 15 or 30 years after that.

There are two main types of forecast: *predictions*, or judgments about the future; and *projections*, which are extrapolations of existing trends into the future. A projection is a conditional statement: it takes the form of saying that 'other things being equal, if we make certain assumptions, this will be true'. A sound projection should identify the conditions explicitly.

Projection

The standard technique in projection is to identify trends in linear form, and to carry the line forward on the basis of the previous trend. The lines are commonly drawn through one of three main techniques:

- using historical data;
- identifying 'moving averages' for previous time periods. Each result in the trend is based on the average of several time periods, rather than a single point. For example, indexes of house prices

or price inflation are issued each month, but refer to the previous year. This smooths out differences in the data;

- using weighted moving averages. The weights make it possible to give more recent time periods greater weight than more distant time periods.

Not many projections in public policy are made just by identifying linear trends. Most complex problems – and practical problems tend to be complex – have several lines to consider, not a single one. *Cohort analysis* assumes that each section of an issue can be projected, and the results can be aggregated to give a total projection. Population forecasting is a relatively straightforward illustration of the problems. Population is predicted by tracking cohorts in a range of age brackets, which makes it possible to predict patterns of fertility, ageing and mortality over time. At a global level, population forecasting is mainly determined by the relationship of births to deaths. If more people die, the population falls; if more people are born, it grows. Deaths are linked to health, and births to fertility. For a large country, like the UK, population is still largely determined by mortality and fertility, but migration plays a visible part. For a city, migration comes to play a larger role. The planning of schooling and old people's homes seems as a matter of common sense to depend on how many children or old people there are; but that will often not be determined by birth or death rates. For any small area, the number of children depends on how many families and people of child-bearing age move into the area. The number of old people, similarly, tends to depend proportionately on what kind of accommodation there is in the area (which encourages old people to move or to remain in an area), and how many younger people move out. Simply put, the smaller the area, the more important migration becomes, and the less important mortality becomes.

Household formation is more complex, because the number of households depends not just on population, but on housing supply, household formation and fission (or break-up), when one household breaks up into two. The national projections for the numbers of households are developed through the following procedures:

- The population is projected, both nationally and sub-nationally.
- Marital status is projected nationally (regional estimates are based on national estimates).

- The institutional population is calculated, and subtracted from the rest of the population.
- Household membership is projected from censuses and the Labour Force Survey.
- The data are then broken down into sub-national areas, and discrepancies are smoothed out.[116]

These figures are surprisingly crude – there is nothing to take into account the effects of economic change, social change or migration. That might help to explain why housebuilding has been subject to such radical under-investment and inconsistent development in the course of the last 30 years.

Parameters and modelling

Projections depend on the assumption that 'other things are equal'. The assumptions behind that statement are referred to as 'parameters'. Parameters are often, wrongly, identified with limits; that is not what the term means. Once parameters have been identified, it should be possible to test what would happen if they were different. These are sometimes called 'what if?' calculations, because they address the question 'what if things were different?'. In the US, they are referred to as 'sensitivity analyses', because they are identifying how sensitive the outcomes are to the assumptions.[117]

A 'model' is a statement about the relationships between different factors. Projections – conditional statements about current trends – tell us what will happen if things continue in the same way. Models tell us what impact the variations in different factors are likely to have. Taking again the example of population, we might assume that, if other things are equal, levels of migration are likely to remain at current levels. Migration is clearly affected, however, by a range of factors, such as the state of the economy. So we can model migration in terms of different rates of economic growth, producing high, medium and low estimates of migration according to the variation of economic conditions. The more factors that are taken into account, the more complex the model becomes. Economic forecasting in the UK depends on a multi-factorial model maintained by the Treasury. Over the years, this model has become progressively more complex and sophisticated; every change in tax or interest rates is passed through the model to see what the likely effects might be.

Models are often expressed as equations, suggesting that each variable is the product of a range of contributory factors. Others can be represented as 'decision trees', where at each stage there are different possible outcomes. A 'Markov model' is a sequence of possible events where the odds of going down each branch of the tree have been calculated. These approaches can be used, for example, to examine possible outcomes from health care treatments.[118] If they are not much used in public policy analysis, however, it is because they assume a level of knowledge and precision about likely outcomes which is rarely available in practice.

Case study: The flow of people with dementia

This case study is taken from a much larger piece of work on planning to meet the needs of people with dementia.[119] Dementia is a progressive illness, mainly affecting people in old age. People who are suffering from dementia do not always know they have it, and sometimes they do not want to know. People pass through a series of stages, but the stages are not very predictable or clearly defined. Currently there are few effective treatments, but as the illness progresses, people are likely to need an increasing input from services, including health, social care and domestic support.

The model which is outlined here is a very simplified version of a 'cohort simulation'. It is based on some very rough assumptions, and it provides indicators, not clear predictions. The assumptions, which are based partly on the literature and partly on a census of older people with dementia in Tayside,[120] were that:

- 60% of people with dementia are in community care, and 40% in residential care;
- 24% of people with dementia die every year;
- 25% of those in the community transfer each year to institutions; and
- the prevalence, or number of cases, is constant. This means that the same number of people are diagnosed with dementia every year as the number of people dying, so that the number of people with dementia does not increase or decrease.

The fourth assumption is the most artificial, and least well-founded. The main reason for making it is that, when in doubt, things have to be assumed to stay the same. The incidence of dementia has been fairly stable up to now,[121] but that does not have to be true in the future. If the incidence changes, so will prevalence.

Once the assumption has been made that the numbers will be relatively stable, other assumptions about the numbers in community or residential care have to be brought into line. The secondary assumptions were as follows:

- New cases occur in the community, rather than in residential care. (This assumption is convenient, but it is not necessarily true. Some people go straight into residential care, without getting support in the community, and their dementia is discovered there. It has also been suggested that the onset of dementia might be accelerated by admission to residential care. If that is right, policy can make a difference to rates of incidence and prevalence.)
- Mortality is higher in residential care than in the community. 15% of people with dementia in the community, and 37.5% of those in institutions, die each year.

Working from these assumptions, Table 6.1 shows what happens to 100 people over four years. By the end of the first year, only 61% of people are in the same position as when they started. After two years, this is 38%.

The next step is to change the parameters – that is, to alter the assumptions, and see what effect the alterations have.

- The central assumption made above was that the size of the pool – the number of people with dementia – would remain constant. If that is not true, it affects the rate of change. Greater incidence or lesser mortality generally would reduce the speed of the flow; greater mortality or lesser incidence would increase it. Mortality of 29%

Table 6.1: The flow of people with dementia (numbers)

	Year 0	Year 1	Year 2	Year 3	Year 4
Community care					
Initial pool	60	36	22	16	11
Year 1 incidence		24	14	8	5
Year 2 incidence			22	14	8
Year 3 incidence				22	14
Year 4 incidence					22
Total	60	60	60	60	60
Residential/institutional care					
Initial pool	40	25	16	10	6
Year 1 intake		15	9	6	4
Year 2 intake			15	9	6
Year 3 intake				15	9
Year 4 intake					15
Total	40	40	40	40	40

Source: P Spicker, DS Gordon, 1997, *Planning for the needs of people with dementia*, Aldershot: Ashgate. Reproduced with permission from Ashgate Publishing.

instead of 24%, depending on its distribution between community and residential care, would bring the figures for those remaining in the same position down to 56% after year 1 and 31% after year 2. Conversely, a mortality rate which was 19% instead of 24% would slow the rate of change, with 66% remaining in the pool after year 1 and 45% after year 2.

- If proportionally more people die while living in the community, or the rate of transfer to residential care alters, the relative figures for residential and community care could alter considerably. Either of these might be true if the provision of residential care changes.
- If people stayed in the community longer, then on these assumptions mortality would fall, and the rate of change would slow down.

Overall, however, it remains true across a wide range of assumptions that most people with dementia will be in a different position after two years. Only one person in six is in the same circumstances after four years.

There are, obviously enough, important limitations to this approach. Dementia is not neatly progressive. Fluctuations in the needs of a population do not necessarily cancel each other out. We cannot say anything from the model about the position of any individual. But the model still has powerful implications for policy. From the point of view of planners, the 'population with dementia' is constantly changing. Service responses which take over two years between planning and implementation – which includes many new projects – have to be addressed not to the problems of people who have dementia now, but to problems which are likely to arise in the future. From the point of view of service delivery, people who have dementia over a long period of time in stable circumstances are untypical. People's needs are likely to change even more rapidly than they do in the model, because they will change while they are in the community, and while they are in residential care. It follows that services need to be geared to people who may have problems for relatively short periods, and the services have to be flexible enough to respond to changing needs.

The implications for policy are not decisive, but they would not be decisive even if the model's predictions were firm and precise. They are based on an interpretation of the situation, and interpretations are always open to alternative readings. The parameters have to be changed very substantially before the outcomes are significantly different. Another way of saying this is that the model is 'robust'. That remains true even if it is not particularly accurate. (The opposite might be true of other case studies – there are models which are so sensitive to their assumptions that no useful prediction can be made. Some caution is needed.)

Prediction

A projection is necessarily a conditional statement. Implicitly, a projection takes the form that 'if this statement is true, then, other things being equal, this is what will happen'. However, other things are rarely equal. The data may seem to show patterns, like oscillations, cycles, growth curves (steeply rising), decline curves (flattening) or 'S' curves (which begin with rapid growth then slow to less rapid growth). It is unwise to project without some element of judgment, and reasoned predictions tend to be more convincing than crude projections. Population forecasting is complex, but it lends itself to projective techniques. For other, less tractable problems – such as economic development or social change – there are other techniques for collating judgments about the future. These do not have to be done quantitatively. The 'Delphi technique' collates individual expert judgments (a different process from inviting discussion between an expert group). Experts are asked individually, and without prior discussion, what they think; their positions are then compared and contrasted.

'Cross–impact analysis' modifies the Delphi technique by putting different influences into a matrix, examining how each factor interacts with the others. This sounds complicated, but it isn't; a 'matrix' is simply a cross–tabulation. If there are four factors to predict, like 'society', 'the economy', 'the population' and 'housing', a matrix is a table with six cells, like this:

			Housing
		Population	
	Economy		
Society			

Respondents have to fill in each of the empty boxes.

Policy analysis, Scriven suggests, is often based around 'scenario evaluation', that is, evaluation of alternative possible futures, each corresponding to a different policy'.[122] 'Scenario building' gives an expert group the opportunity to examine their assumptions qualitatively. There is an example of scenario building in the Wanless Report on the NHS. Wanless was asked to look at 'technological, demographic and medical trends' over the course of 20 years. As part of that exercise, the inquiry constructed three scenarios:

- solid progress, with increasing life expectancy, service targets being met and a background of improving social conditions;
- slow uptake, with increasing long-term chronic illness, slow implementation of new technologies and limited change in service use;
- full engagement, with improving public health and improving service.[123]

None of these scenarios raises major concerns about the viability of the NHS.

Although predictions may seem on the face of the matter to be more subjective, and possibly less 'scientific', than projections are, the arguments for preferring predictions are good ones. Projections depend heavily on the assumptions that are made. Predictions depend on judgments about the strength of those assumptions and the influence of external factors. Taking this kind of information into account makes predictions vaguer and less certain than projections, but they can also be more sound.

Exercise

Review local population forecasts from a housing strategy or structure plan. What would happen if the estimates of migration were 20% out?

SEVEN

Methods, constraints and resources

Selecting methods is, properly speaking, part of policy formation, but understanding the process is also important for policy review. In practice, Scriven suggests, policy analysis is often concerned with things that have not actually happened – alternative approaches which might have been taken, the things that might go wrong, or the ways that policies might be adapted in the future.[124] The role of the policy analyst in the process of policy development is not always clear – it has to be discussed and negotiated. By the time an analysis gets under way, both the methods and the institutional structure are likely to be decided on, and analysis has to respond to the consequences of the arrangement, not to offer 'blue sky' solutions. There may be scope to negotiate some changes, but it is likely to be limited. Understanding approaches to method is important partly because it helps to explain where policies might have gone wrong, and where they might still go wrong, but also partly because making recommendations about developing or improving a policy calls for an understanding of how else things might be done.

Government action

The kinds of action which can be taken depend on the powers and competence of the organisation which does them. Central government in the UK is legally unrestricted in most of the actions it can take (although there are treaty obligations, particularly relating to the European Union, which limit the potential course of action). Central government in many other countries, like the US or the Federal Republic of Germany, is limited by a constitution or basic law: governments can only do what they are permitted to do. (For over a century, local government in the UK has been allowed to do only those things which are expressly permitted by law: other actions are 'ultra vires', or beyond its powers, and cannot be undertaken legitimately. This limitation has been relaxed recently through the creation of a general power to promote well-being, but local authorities have not used this power much yet.) Most autonomous and quasi-autonomous public sector organisations have a constitution which defines the legitimate range of action open to them.

Governments have access to a wide range of tools and methods. In the popular mind, much of what governments do takes the form of coercion. That is because many of the most visible forms of intervention – taxation, road traffic control and criminal law – are compulsory. But this is not typical of most public action. The patterns of government action are not confined to making other people do things; states have the option to undertake tasks themselves, for example through direct service provision, military intervention or purchasing services. The basic methods for changing the pattern of what other people do are:

- regulation;
- coercion;
- provision;
- persuasion;
- promotion; and
- planning.

Regulation. Regulation is basic to government activity. States establish the rules under which other social actors, including individuals, groups, companies and organisations, operate. They establish the structures and frameworks which determine people's formal relationships – both at a personal level, in such things as marriage and parental rights, and institutionally, in such structures as a limited liability company or a charity. They can use regulation to prevent or exclude options from this framework – like polygamy or business cartels. They may also be able to develop new structures: for example, local authorities may develop community enterprises and partnerships to achieve political or economic objectives. The European Union has relied on regulation as a primary means of developing its influence in social policy, to the point where it has been described as a 'regulatory state'.[125]

Despite the importance of regulation as a policy instrument, there is very limited scope for it in the kinds of settings where most policy analysts work. The reason is that new regulations are likely to need primary legislation, and that takes time and resources which are not available in the short term. It is usually more realistic to think in terms of enforcing the rules which exist, and even that may not be possible.

Coercion. Coercion is sometimes assumed to be at the root of what governments do,[126] but it is not straightforward, and when it is examined in more detail the concept fragments into a diverse range of different kinds of approaches. It includes both negative sanctions for actions which are forbidden, like the criminal law, and mandatory rules like taxation or compulsory education. Because governments have a variety of coercive tools in their armoury, it is often sufficient to apply pressure, or to suggest at coercion, rather than go all the way. The essence of coercion rests in the application of a sanction for non-compliance. The effect of a sanction should be sufficient to forestall the option − making it effectively non-eligible − as opposed, say, to taxing an activity, which simply makes it less eligible than previously. Freedom depends on the number and range of options which are available to a person.[127] Whether or not sanctions are coercive, consequently, depends on context. Forbidding actions is coercive if the remaining options offer only a restricted course of action. Banning broadcasts on unlicensed radio stations could, in some circumstances, be seen as a major assault on civil liberties, but it is largely accepted in the UK because there are so many other options for public expression. Making actions permissible only on condition − like possession of a driving licence − is usually seen as regulatory, rather than coercive, probably because authorisation is available under certain conditions. The same is not true of some other restrictions, such as the use of narcotics, because the conditions for authorisation are much more restrictive.

As with regulation, the scope for coercion in practical policy making tends to be very limited. In England, Anti-Social Behaviour Orders, or ASBOs, have brought powers of coercion down to a local level, which has created new opportunities to stop people doing things, but it is still early to say what the scope of the coercive powers will be. Even where coercion is possible, like the possibility of levying local charges or requiring children to wear safety helmets, there may still be a risk of non-compliance. It should always be assumed that rules are liable to be broken.

Provision. Governments are able to supply and distribute services directly, either by organising and paying for delivery, or by co-opting the necessary labour to achieve them. The NHS is a classic example. At a local level, one obvious way to provide a service is to hire someone to do it − becoming an employer. If the function falls within the remit of an existing service, the appointment can be made within that service; if it cannot, it may be necessary to establish a project, 'programme' or special office to do it. Alternatively, one of the options open to any organisation is to pay suppliers to achieve the effects it wants to bring about – water supply, transport routes or health care. Public sector organisations can purchase specific services.

Persuasion. Persuasion (or dissuasion) may take the form of government-sponsored education, propaganda, advertising and other means of opinion-forming – including, potentially, lies, indoctrination, state-sponsored religions and even the appointment of a personal advisor to give people the correct answer. (The last example may seem far-fetched, but it was the model for maternity visitors, now health visitors, after 1919.) The development of public health in the past 30 years has come to rely less on regulation and coercion (for example through slum clearance and food regulation), and increasingly on education and health promotion.[128]

Persuasion is not more likely to work than other forms of policy instrument, but there is a certain naivety in some policy initiatives – the assumption that, if something is promoted, that is what will happen. There is no reason to believe, for example, that people who have been told that having sex is a bad idea are likely not to have it, and it is difficult to view the US government's current sponsorship of sexual abstinence programmes as a serious attempt to develop effective policy.

Promotion. Promotion, where it means more than persuasion, refers to the use of rewards to encourage forms of action. Government subsidy is a form of government promotion of activity: it can act either to reduce the costs of undertaking an activity, or to increase its benefits. The converse of promotion is deterrence, which implies discouragement of action by increasing costs, or reducing benefits; taxation can be used in this way. The primary strategy in the UK for the reduction of smoking, for example, has been a combination of public health education (persuasion) with deterrent taxation.

This can be linked to financial methods, including subsidy and incentive. Subsidies are payments for services where the supply is determined not by the purchaser but by a beneficiary (for example, private householders who are subsidised to insulate their dwellings, or health care consumers in France who are partly reimbursed for their pharmaceutical costs) or the supplier (for example, subsidies given to transport services to ensure that certain levels of service are maintained). Subsidies have become less common in recent years than they were, partly because they are considered less discriminating than purchasing arrangements, but also because they are considered to distort the functioning of the market and as such breach European Union rules.

The idea of 'incentives' is drawn from economics, where the purpose is to consider effects on aggregate behaviour. It does not follow, in economics, that an inducement will lead either to a particular individual response, or even that it will lead to a uniform aggregate response. That depends on aggregate responsiveness, or 'elasticity'. Incentives and disincentives work by affecting some of the population, so that aggregates increase or diminish in response to an incentive or disincentive. Incentive policies are concerned with change at the margins, not with fundamental morality. Many government policies are concerned with the direction of movement, not the uniform behaviour of each and every person: this is most obviously true in economics, but it applies no less in many social areas, like education or family life. Incentive policies are an obvious way of attempting to direct the course of a population. An incentive can be a single carrot for a thousand donkeys, like a prize competition. If we want to encourage 'enterprise', to develop scientific education, or to support sporting hopefuls, for example, we do not need to change the behaviour of every individual: we only need to change a few. (This is not the way that incentives and disincentives are often represented in the literature – many commentators, working on a 'rational choice' model, assume that incentives act as rewards or punishments for each individual.[129] This does not have much to do with economics, and rewards and punishments are aspects of coercion rather than incentive policy.)

Planning. Planning is an odd collection of all these methods, and more. Planning is simply strategic politics, and political negotiation may consist of a combination of bargaining, reasoning, bluster, bribery, education, pleading, blackmail and threat in pursuit of political ends. Several European governments work on a 'corporatist' model, structuring the roles of a range of agencies within the framework of the government's priorities.[130]

This is not an exhaustive account. Governments could, for example, compete economically with private enterprise, or conscript labour, but few do so. The list reviewed here serves to illustrate two main points. The first is diversity. Governments have a huge range of different options open to them in pursuit of their political aims. This is much more limited at the level of local government. Central government has the power to legislate; local government is generally confined both in terms of central regulation, and in practice through a limited power to affect the economic, social and legal context in which it operates. Because regulation and coercion are not available, they tend to have to rely on persuasion, promotion and planning.

The second is the limitations of government behaviour. The diversity of options reflects the difficulty which governments have in achieving their ends through straightforward compulsion. Whether it is for moral reasons or practical ones, governments do not simply announce that from tomorrow the world will be different. Those governments which have tried to do so have generally failed. The French revolution attempted to abolish the calendar, the system of weights and measures and the Catholic Church. (Only the system of weights and measures stuck.) The Bolshevik revolution attempted to abolish the institution of marriage, without any great success. Like King Canute ordering back the waves, government pronouncements about teenage pregnancy or drug abuse often seem to ignore the limits of their competence. In fairness to Canute, it has been said that he staged the incident to show his courtiers that he was not superhuman. It is not clear that the governments of the UK or the US have a similar moral lesson in mind.

On doing nothing

One of the most important options for policy has not been considered in this list. Governments do not necessarily have to do anything at all. They can leave things as they are; they can refuse to intervene; they can withdraw from intervention. There are two different kinds of argument nested together here, and they need to be unravelled. The first kind of argument is political or ideological. It starts from the premise that there is a presumption against government intervention. Libertarians, like Nozick[131] and Hayek,[132] argue for a minimal role for government; any state which intervenes actively infringes people's freedom, and that can be justified only in a limited range of circumstances. Free-marketeers, like Friedman, argue that markets provide a better way of doing things.[133] The advice of HM Treasury on policy accepts this basic proposition when it discusses the 'rationale' for policy;[134] policy makers are asked to begin from the assumption that intervening is only clearly justified when there are commonly recognised problems in market distribution. Examples include public goods, when certain types of activity like parks and sewers have a public character which is not reflected in the way that the markets determine value and distribution, or 'market failure', where problems like imperfect information and monopoly supply distort the operation of the market.

The second kind of argument is particular to policy analysis. The null option – the question of what would happen if nothing is done – is often needed to work out what effect a policy has; and a sense of what happens if 'other things are equal' is crucial for policies which depend on models. Policy analysts routinely have to consider what the effects of non-intervention might be, even when non-intervention is not genuinely being considered as a policy option.

Case study: Social inclusion in France

The idea of 'social inclusion' has been a framework for a range of methods to be applied, responding to poverty, unemployment and a range of social problems. The idea originated in France. France has had no tradition of referring to 'poverty' in the development of social policy. Social welfare provision has been seen to depend primarily on the Catholic idea of 'solidarity' or mutual responsibility: the *Code de Sécurité Sociale* states that solidarity is its central principle.[135] When René Lenoir wrote, in the early 1970s, about people who had been left out of the French social security system, he referred to them as *Les exclus*, the 'excluded'.[136] Initially, exclusion was taken to refer to people who were not part of the networks of social solidarity which were available to everyone else.

The idea of 'inserting' the excluded is at the root of the introduction of the *Revenu Minimum d'Insertion* (RMI), introduced in 1988. The RMI combines a basic, means-tested benefit with provision for a 'contract of insertion' made between the claimant and the local authority, the *Commission Locale d'Insertion* (CLI). The CLI, in turn, has an obligation to make arrangements with providers and employers in order to create opportunities for insertion. The 1988 law made the following provisions:

Art. 36

In the three months which follow the beginning of the payment of benefit, there is established between the benefit agency (allocataire) and the persons [who claim] ... a contract of insertion, which will take into account

- all elements that are useful for appreciating their health, social, professional, financial and housing situation of the interested parties;
- the nature of the project of insertion that they are able to form or which can be put to them;
- the nature of the facilities which can be offered to them to help them realise this project;
- the timetable of steps and activities of insertion implied for the realisation of the project.

> *Art. 37*
>
> The insertion proposed to the beneficiaries of the RMI and agreed with them can, in particular, take the form
>
> - of activities for the collective interest in an administration, a social service, or a society which is non-profit making;
> - of activities or courses of insertion in a professional setting;
> - of courses intended for the acquisition or improvement of a professional qualification by the interested parties;
> - of actions intended to help the beneficiaries to refind or to develop their social independence.

The process of making these contracts is not universally respected: the CLIs are dealing with a shifting population, who are not necessarily going to want or need detailed support. There are some localities where the view taken of contracts is very limited. I visited one commune where the contracts were seen almost wholly in terms of employment; in another, where there were very few options for employment, almost none were. What has been interesting about the RMI has been the variety of methods and approaches.

The pattern of contracts has been characterised generally in terms of three main types of insertion: social, professional and economic.[137] Social insertion refers to the situation of people who are excluded by virtue of social disadvantage, for example disability or single parenthood. Contracts can include courses in literacy, parental education, budgeting and managing housing. Professional insertion is for people who require some kind of training or preparation for work. This includes training and professional courses, pre-qualification courses, and 'motivation'. Economic insertion is for people who are unemployed but who would be in a position to move directly to employment. Examples include contracts for seeking employment, starting a business, and 'employment-solidarity' (job creation).[138] Action for insertion and formation (AIF) includes programmes of training and counselling selected for individuals: according to Dugué and Maillard, 'it brings together all the provisions for overview, evaluation, motivation and *formation* (training and education) appropriate to the needs of each individual'.[139]

Even in cases where methods adopted seem to be inventive and almost unfettered, there are important constraints. First, the powers of any agency can only go so far: social policies are constrained by economics, local policies are constrained by national ones. Second, there is sometimes a failure of implementation: the process of forming contracts has been limited by low take-up, reservations by the social workers responsible for negotiating the contracts, and the concerns of claimants. Third, the options are blinkered by pre-set patterns of thought; the heavy emphasis on employment and economic insertion in some places means it can be difficult to distinguish the RMI from 'workfare'.

> The contract expresses the wish to maintain a direct link between work and obtaining resources.... There is a largish consensus in relation to this ancient idea, provided that it is kitted out in the latest fashion. It could have been taken up equally well by the right as by the left.[140]

The French approach has been profoundly influential in the European Union. Benefit systems based on the RMI have been introduced in Belgium and Portugal, and parts of Spain and Italy. One of the main critiques of the system, however, must be that the range of methods has not been wide enough. The contract of insertion brings responsibility down to the level of the individual; but unemployment and poverty are also the product of economic conditions and the social structure. *RMIstes* complain that they are being treated as deviant, when what they need is work.

> Most of the beneficiaries do not recognise themselves in the terms 'excluded' or 'marginal'. They have no work and they want it, even if they know, for the most part, that they will not find it.[141]

Constraints

The range of methods which is considered has to be the range of methods which are possible. In practice, decisions are constrained by many factors. This section considers the more common ones.

Values and ideology. Some methods are likely to be discounted out of hand, possibly because they are considered and rejected as unacceptable, but possibly because patterns of thought are so firmly set that other options are not even thought about. For example, the assumption that children must have two parents has shaped policy decisions about adoption, child care, the rights of subsequent partners and child support. The same assumption is not made in other jurisdictions.[142] Bachrach and Baratz coined the term 'non-decision' to refer to the issues that are not on the table, and to decisions that are not even made because they are so obviously unthinkable.[143]

Legal constraints. Constitutional and administrative law defines what it is possible to take into account, and what is not. There may be constitutional limitations on the power or authority of public services: powers (or 'competences') have to be granted legally. Many of the debates in social policy in the European Union have been about establishing the powers of the Union in areas like public health or social exclusion. Establishing the principle has often been more important than the specific issue: it has led to bitter debates about bus passes for pensioners (competence in the welfare of old people and in public transport), language teaching in schools (competence in education) and the effect of aluminium in water supplies on workers needing renal dialysis (competence in environmental health). In the UK, the kinds of legal constraints that are likely to have an influence are limitations (real or feared) about Data Protection or Human Rights legislation, and specific rules introduced to govern policy areas.

In Chapter One, I mentioned one of the legal principles that every administrator ought to be aware of: natural justice. Natural justice has two central elements: that decisions about disputes have to hear evidence from both sides, and that because decisions have to be seen to be fair, arbitrators have to be free of compromising interests.[144] These principles run through lots of issues in practice: they govern issues like dispute resolution, disciplinary hearings and the declaration of interests by decision makers. Another important principle, more recently introduced than natural justice but no less important for administrative practice, is promissory estoppel.[145] Subject to the powers of the agency, it says that if an official makes a statement, and that people act on the strength of that statement, the agency is bound by the consequences. Natural justice and promissory estoppel are core principles, and even if some agencies or administrators choose to ignore them, the courts won't.

External policies. It is not uncommon for governments to adopt general policies, with the intention that they should be used as a test for later decisions. Examples are environmental policies, such as Agenda 21 and environmental impact assessments,[146] or mainstreaming policies on gender.[147] This sort of approach is unlikely in itself to lead to material changes in policy, but it does give advocates of the issues within decison-making bodies the opportunity to raise concerns formally. It follows that they are more likely to act as an obstacle to inconsistent actions than a positive force for change.

Administrative constraints. Administration ought to be workable, and the observation that an agency does not have the capacity to implement the policy ought to be viewed as a serious objection. Policy makers ignore this at their peril; several major administrative fiascoes have happened largely because decision makers chose to disregard the warnings. The computerisation of social security has led to repeated, predictable problems because of the determination to produce an all-singing, all-dancing computer program that would do everything. It sounds like a good idea to link fields and records in a common, accessible store, but this is the Holy Grail of information technology projects – computers cannot store correspondence and phone calls from users effectively, which means there always have to be multiple files. The Child Support Agency in the UK, another example in a similar field, tried to replace a previous, unsatisfactory system with an assessment that relied on an impossibly complex means test – requiring information about the income, household circumstances and relative liabilities of two parents living in different households. Any of these elements would be difficult; balancing all six made the task unworkable.

Path dependency. The way things have been done is a major constraint on the ways that things can be done in the future. This tends to be seen as a form of inertia, and there is some truth in the idea that policy which is not deliberately changed will carry on unless some other force intervenes. This has been translated, in political science, into the idea of 'path dependency': that policy travels on tramlines, and once things have started, they can be difficult to stop. An example might be pensions. Pensions are not policies for a single point in time; they are based in the past, the present and the future. In the past, people will have made contributions, and have gained entitlements. In the present, current pensioners have needs and problems, conditioned by previous policies, which any policy has to address. Current contributors, meanwhile, are changing their behaviour, and gaining entitlements, which will affect their position in the future, and commit agencies which will deal with them.

Path dependency can be interrupted by major events, like wars, natural catastrophes or economic collapse, but policy cannot be planned on that basis. Changing policy for pensions is a long-term operation. It requires consideration of established entitlements, current needs and future expectations. Transitional arrangements may have to be put in place. It may take 20 years or more to bring about major changes.

The attitudes of administrators and officials. There are many ways in which reforms can be 'tripped up' by officials. Stoker refers both to 'exploitation' or opportunistic behaviour – taking advantage of administrative change to bring about shifts in approach, function or policy – and to direct antagonism.[148] If officials really do not want to do something, they can say 'no' in more languages than there are in the continent of Africa. Some of the reasons for not doing things are listed by Perri 6 and his colleagues.[149] They include:

- lacking the authority, including legal constraints, contractual agreements, data protection, and so on;
- lacking legitimacy, on the basis that policy is not delivering tangible benefits, or the proposal comes from an unrepresentative source;
- lacking the capacity, including resources, management capacity, and so on;
- low priority, because existing tasks are more important;
- fear of loss of control, including the effects on professional power and career opportunities;
- bargaining, where agreement is conditional on other steps being taken;
- jeopardy, where it is argued that there are risks and dangers in the policy;
- inconsistency with objectives, including the accusations that policy is contradictory and will not work; and
- difficulty, because of the problems of methods, implementation or practicality.

I pointed earlier to the dangers of disregarding administrative experience. In fairness, that has to be set against the possibility that administrators might just be finding ways of putting obstacles in the way. David Donnison, formerly the Chair of the Supplementary Benefits Commission, comments wrily that when the civil servants were reduced to objecting that there weren't enough filing cabinets to do the job he wanted, he knew he had them on the run.[150] Perri 6 and his colleagues comment: 'it became clear from our case studies that when it is hard to do something, it is more usually because they do not want to rather than because they cannot.... In general, 'can't' turns out to mean 'won't'.[151]

Financial constraints. Finance is central to many decisions. Almost every decision has an opportunity cost – there is something else that could be done with the same resources. If a measure costs too much, or if it does not seem to deliver value for money, the decision is likely to be reviewed and trimmed. These issues are considered further in the next chapter.

Resources

The section on 'constraints' is framed negatively – it considers the issues that stop methods from being adopted. However, there is another way to represent the same issues. A constraint is a limitation on what is possible. It is also, however, a point which defines what is possible. Financial resources, for example, identify what can be spent; staffing complements, how many people are available to fulfil defined tasks, and how much time they have. The key resources include:

- *Finance.* Some money is always tied up – committed to particular purposes, like salaries or buildings. But money which is available for one purpose can often be spent in a different way. One standard way of reviewing methods is to ask how else the money could be used, whether more resources might make new methods possible, or whether diverting money to another approach might be appropriate.
- *Accommodation.* Buildings which are used for one purpose can often be used for another, either by a reallocation of space or by rethinking the role of the service. Many housing departments have converted residential units in difficult-to-let areas to service bases for community organisations. A youth service I did some work with converted half its office space into a drop-in centre and cafeteria.
- *Staff.* The time of workers is one of the principal resources available to an agency. A typical office worker spends about 1,600 hours each year at work. Time spent in one way can often be spent in another, and the hours spent at work can be sub-divided and allocated differently. Changing people's functions is often difficult; it can make staff feel unskilled and insecure. But it can also be a way of recognising expertise and drawing on competence. Wardens in sheltered housing were initially charged with janitorial functions in developments and protecting vulnerable people in the event of accident. As time went on, it came to be appreciated that many of the things that wardens were doing – providing personal support and organising social activities – were at least as valuable, if not more so.
- *Knowledge and information.* Many agencies are sitting on a mine of information – and indeed, drawing on the existing stock of information is the staple currency of policy analysis. It is typically

the basis for the assessment of the environment, the development of indicators and the definition of targets.

- *Service users.* The time, expertise and commitment of service users are often a major resource. This ranges from voluntary engagement and service work to formal participation, and from that to institutional engagement at senior levels.

Case study: Responding to child abuse

The prevention of child abuse is another area in which a range of methods can be used, but responses have to be formed within a legal and moral framework that obstructs intervention, and they are subject to considerable constraints on resources. Concern with child abuse is a surprisingly recent innovation. Child abuse has almost certainly been a problem for centuries, but it has not been a social problem; it was nobody else's business. The neglect of children became an offence under the 1868 Poor Law Amendment Act; neglect was considered an issue because some parents refused to support their families, making them a burden on the parish. Abandonment, rather than maltreatment, was the main source of public concern. Largely through the efforts of the National Society for the Prevention of Cruelty to Children, cruelty was also identified as an issue, and their efforts led to the 1889 Prevention of Cruelty to Children Act, the first legislation of its kind. Maternity visiting, introduced after the First World War, meant that nearly all new mothers were visited by a trained midwife. The 1933 Children and Young Persons Act greatly extended penalties for cruelty and abuse. It is not true to say, then, that there was no awareness of child abuse. What is true is that awareness was limited and not considered to be a major problem. When evidence of child abuse was 'discovered' in the US in the 1950s, many people, including professionals, refused to believe it. It took the scientific evidence of radiologists, who were able to show patterns of fractures by X-rays, to persuade an unbelieving medical profession that parents were capable of sustained physical abuse of their children. A similar reaction followed the discovery of sexual abuse of children, now very much recognised as part of a recurring pattern of abuse.

Intervention to deal with child abuse developed equally slowly. The 1948 Children Act gave local authorities in England and Wales the power to take children into care in the event of child abuse. This was a very limited power, and pressure from the appointed officials (the 'Children's Officers') led to an extension of powers in 1952, to allow local authorities to *investigate* cases of abuse. It was not until 1963 that local authorities gained the power to take action to *prevent* child abuse. The methods used were mainly developed by voluntary organisations, notably the Family Support Unit, which pioneered the approach we now recognise as social work with children and families.

The constraints affecting work to prevent child abuse are very considerable. They include:

- *values and ideology.* Prevention takes place within a strong moral framework supporting families. In a perceptive pamphlet, Sheppard notes that the scope of potential interventions is greatly limited by convention.[152] When people talk about the problem of child abuse, they assume that it represents deviant or incompetent behaviour. No-one suggests that children should not routinely be raised by their parents. No-one is seriously arguing for state-run nurseries, or a test of competence before parents are allowed to raise children. More strikingly, because it is a much more serious proposition, at the time Sheppard was writing hardly anyone had tried to make any link between child abuse and the physical punishment of children – a link which, in the course of the past 20 years, has become accepted by virtually every main organisation working in the field of child care.

  The presumption in favour of the family is a fundamental constraint on the work it is possible to undertake. Workers in child abuse are frequently criticised for intervening too actively – as they were, for example, in Cleveland, where paediatricians dared to diagnose in cases referred to them for confirmation, or Orkney, where children were removed from their homes after unambiguous, cross-corroborated accounts of sexual abuse in ritual settings. But they are equally criticised for inaction, not only in cases where they have been misled or have failed to gain access to children, but in cases where they have tried to keep the family intact.

- *legal constraints.* Social workers have very few legal powers, and precious few resources. Their ability to negotiate interventions with families consequently depends largely on a combination of their ability to 'read' their clients, moral pressure, the fear of imagined consequences and sales technique.

- *administrative problems.* A consistent feature of child abuse scandals has been a picture of social work as understaffed, overburdened, unable to mount effective responses because there are simply too many people to visit and too few people to do it. Preventative work is time-consuming and uncertainly effective. If services have to be rationed, the implications of reducing time and contact are not clear or direct; many services, of necessity, take the risk.

- *uncertainty.* Social work with families is all about risk – a sense of what might happen, rather than the confident knowledge that it will. Much depends on the assessment of individual cases – assessing not only what the current position is, but also how that situation is likely to develop.

Despite the limitations, the range of options for action is still very varied. There is no single, fixed pattern of social work with families; social workers begin with an assessment of circumstances and try to find an appropriate response in context. Typical methods include:

- responses to personal problems, including 'psychodynamic' approaches (talking through problems), non-directive counselling, education and groupwork;
- family-based approaches, like family therapy, mediation, conciliation and contract work (making contracts with family members); and
- approaches dealing with people in their social context, including advocacy, material support (for example, housing and welfare rights), community education and community organisation.

Any of these methods might work at some times and not at others. Applying them effectively depends strongly on selecting an appropriate method and being able to use it in context. Social work is a thankless task. Successes do not attract much attention; if everything works as it should, the family will live a reasonably unremarkable life. Failures, by contrast, attract a great deal of attention; there has been a long series of scandals and inquiries where support has not been delivered adequately, and a child has died.

Decisions about methods

It is difficult to present material on the selection of methods systematically, because so many of the considerations are ad hoc and diffuse. The rational model of policy making suggests that policy makers should review all the alternatives. No-one can do that; information is costly, the effects are unpredictable, and it takes too long. What happens, necessarily, is unsystematic: decision makers will select methods from a small handful of narrowly defined alternatives.

Consistency with aims

Decisions about methods often begin in the wrong place. A lot of people in services have knives and forks, and they are looking for something to cut. For example, whenever there is a disaster, or an atrocity, someone is sure to say: 'these people need counselling'.[153]

Counselling is a method – its efficacy is disputed,[154] but it is fairly carefully worked out, developed and sophisticated[155] – which may or may not be right for the problems in hand. Beginning with the methods, rather than what the methods are supposed to do, is sloppy thinking. The first question to ask is what the aims of a policy are. The second is how the methods relate to those aims.

The vagueness that bedevils the process of developing aims consequently presents problems here. If policy makers do not know what they are supposed to be doing, it can be difficult to justify the methods they use. This is sometimes side-stepped by a circular argument – the aim of a service is to do something specific, like providing education or social work, so that is what service providers will do. Where agencies get the opportunity to develop new services, they tend to do it in ways they understand. So, when social services departments take over day nurseries, they are likely to see it as part of support for families with relationship difficulties, and when education departments take on community development, they have tended to interpret it as 'community education', which is a distinctive style of community work. The methods drive the statement of aims.

Some methods, equally, are seen as aims in themselves. Some policy makers begin from an established set of values and approaches – an 'ideology' – which leads them towards particular types of solution.[156] The 'free market' approaches of the radical right are probably most familiar,[157] but in their way the commitments to participative discussion and partnership working favoured by the World Bank are just as ideological – that is, based in an interrelated system of values and beliefs.

Some decisions are conditioned by established processes, like strategy formation, consultative processes or programme budgeting, and by the instruments available to put policy into practice, like the organisational capacity of agencies or the methods used by professionals. There are likely to be compromises about the methods adopted, and areas of negotiation. The process by which decisions are made is likely to affect the character of the decisions. Although the distinctions cannot be drawn very clearly, there may be important differences between, for example, decisions about method which are made through a bureaucratic structure (such as the DWP, or some parts of the NHS), those which are determined through consensual processes, like local authority partnerships, and those which have been subject to user involvement and participation. As a very rough proposition, policies which are developed taking into account many voices can be expected to be less sharply defined, and less orderly, than those which are not.

Taking into account a range of views is likely to mean that competing issues and perspectives will have been expressed; that there will have been negotiations, and that there may be some compromises; that even if not much has been done to change the policy, there will be some softening of the presentation of the policy; and that the policy has had to be framed in ways which are more likely to satisfy different stakeholders and constituencies. It is difficult to say how far the policy will be substantively different by the end of the process, but policy proposals from traditional, unitary departments look and feel different from other proposals coming from departments committed to partnership and consultation.

Operationalising the methods

Methods, like aims, problems and issues, have to be operationalised – they have to be translated into terms that are capable of being put into practice. The most basic question to be answered is, 'how do we do this?'. There are some methods – like getting money to people, getting them housed, or getting children to school – which serve several purposes at once, and it is possible that one method might be enough to deal with several issues at the same time. However, one policy rarely fits everyone. For example, providing for homeless people is not just a matter of supplying them with houses, as was once thought: there are sub-groups with greater needs, such as young people without other means of support, patients discharged from psychiatric care, and people fleeing domestic violence, and ignoring the distinctions can vitiate the rest of the work done by a housing service. The problems and issues have to be analysed in enough detail to make the selection of appropriate methods possible.

The standard way to deal with complex problems is to break them down into smaller, less complex, problems, and keep on breaking them down, until the problems that are left are small enough to be manageable. An example might be the process of assessing needs for community care. The system of community care is based on individual needs assessments, which are the basis of service responses. There are assessments undertaken for different client groups (elderly people, people with disabilities, people with a learning disability, people with mental health problems, and so on), and for sub-groups. Assessments have to be done differently in different settings – someone in hospital cannot be assessed in the same way as someone in their own home. There are different types of need – such as developmental, physical, financial, social, medical needs or needs for domestic support – which require different types of questions to be asked, and different kinds of expertise to be assessed adequately. And there are issues to consider in the process of assessment, including service coordination, the division of labour between professionals, information management, and linking assessments to resource provision. There has been a persistent problem in this process of service users facing multiple, overlapping assessments from different sources. One of the curses of work in this area has been the religion of 'holistic' assessment, favoured in the training of nurses, health visitors and social workers among others; if everyone is identifying all the problems, the unfortunate client has to go through the same stuff time after time. Effective responses depend on a division of labour between professionals, not on each person duplicating the work of every other person.[158] This is a complex set of relationships, and managing it calls for careful identification of the component elements. Depressingly, however, recent policy has been moving in the direction of greater complexity – trying to deal with everyone through the same, uniform process, a 'Single Shared Assessment', without recognising the reasons why the constituent assessments are done in the first place. The new 'unified' procedure is complex, massively time-consuming and demanding of resources, and other assessments still have to be done.

A second basic question, beyond how things can be done, is what might go wrong. Policy analysis of methods should be able, not just to anticipate predictable problems, but to decide how to cope with unpredictable ones. There needs to be some assessment of how the method will bear up when things change. The technical term for this is 'robustness', but it is 'robust' in a slightly different sense from the usual meaning of that term in social science. A robust method is one that can be adapted to changing circumstances, that will survive despite problems and emergencies or, more simply, that can stand up to battering. A robust policy might be based on a single robust method, but it might also include a policy which gives the agency the chance to adapt – for example, trying several methods, and throwing out those that do not seem to work – or to back out. It may be advisable for an agency to pick an inferior method which does not commit them too deeply. For example, a local authority might choose to fund a welfare rights worker working out of the agency's main office, rather than setting up, for roughly the same cost, a local welfare rights service where the worker is situated closer to the people who are being served. The first of these two options has one main advantage – the worker will be easier to supervise, and can be part of a team – along with clear disadvantages – the worker will spend less time on the job, and more time travelling. The second option is almost certainly a better way to achieve the aims. It will improve access and take-up of the service – the general experience of advice services is that most people come from a limited geographical area. But the first option does not imply any future commitment to maintain specialised accommodation, it can easily be adapted to circumstances, it makes it possible to allocate the worker's time differently, and it can be scrapped at short notice. None of these is true of the second option, and that is why the first is more likely to be chosen.

Effective policy making

Analytical judgments about methods are made on the basis that a method should be *effective* – that is, it should produce the intended effects. There are two main schools of thought about how to assess this. One is a rationalist approach: methods work best when they make sense in relation to the issues. There should be a causal relationship between the problems and issues which are identified, on the one hand, and the methods which are adopted on the other. If, for example, one believes that unemployment breeds crime (which is arguable but not at all clear[159]), tackling unemployment becomes a 'rational' way to tackle crime. In its statement of policy on teenage pregnancy, the UK government has taken the view that having sex leads to babies, so the central issue is to educate young girls about contraception.[160] But the example points to the dangers of jumping to conclusions. Teenage mothers tend to tell researchers that they have made a positive choice; they are not having babies by accident.[161] Sex is necessary to have babies, but it is not sufficient; most people who have sex do not have babies. The next stage is not motherhood, but pregnancy. Pregnancy, like sex, is a necessary condition, but it is also not sufficient; many girls who become pregnant in their teens do not have the baby. There is a huge class differential in the decision to become a teenage mother.[162] Middle-class girls who have the prospect of an education and career tend to choose not to have the baby; by contrast, girls from poorer backgrounds, for whom the best prospect is family life, choose to have the baby. The 'common-sense' assumption that we know what the causal process is is often misguided.

'Primary prevention' works by identifying what the causes of a problem are, and stopping them before they start. The central problem with strategies based on primary prevention is that they might not be addressing the true cause at all. An inadequate analysis of the causal relationships runs the risk that it will lead to the choice of the wrong method, and unfortunately, the causal analysis of complex social issues is nearly always inadequate. Anthony Giddens once wrote:

> The more we understand about why poverty remains widespread, the more likely it is that successful policies can be implemented to counter it.[163]

Prudently, he dropped the comment in later editions of the same book. Understanding poverty – or claiming to understand it – has not led to more successful policies. On the contrary, people who think they understand the causes of poverty are often deluded, and sometimes dangerous. Examples include the advocates of eugenics, which was used to justify sterilisation of the poor;[164] pundits in the US, who have promoted policies which blame the poor for their poverty, as justification for punishment or forced labour;[165] right-wing economists arguing for 'structural adjustment', a process which has plunged some developing countries into economic crisis;[166] and quasi-Marxists who have refused to do anything at all because it couldn't possibly work.[167] The basic problem with most causal statements is that the kinds of association they rely on are complex, multi-faceted and difficult to predict. In practice, Pawson and Tilley argue, policies hardly ever work or don't work; they work for some people, under some conditions, in some circumstances. They argue, on that basis, for a greater emphasis on refining theories, identifying the causal relationships more reliably and accurately.[168] But it goes wrong so often that we might just as reasonably conclude that there is something wrong with the attempt to choose methods and approaches on the basis of rational explanations for complex causal phenomena.

Pawson and Tilley make a key distinction between mechanisms and outcomes. Most people, when they talk about causes, mean them to refer to the reasons why something happens – an outline of a process, or, in Pawson and Tilley's phrase, a 'generative mechanism'. But a cause is also something which has effects or outcomes. The great strength of sociological approaches has not been in identifying mechanisms – explaining the reasons why things happen – but in identifying relationships and associations within a complex mass of data – describing what is actually happening. When items are consistently associated, we can plausibly infer a causal link even if we do not know what the mechanism is. A classic example is the relationship between inequality and ill health[169] – there are many competing explanations for the link, but the association is well enough established to drive policy. The relationship between cause and effect is not, in itself, an explanation of a process: it is a description of what happens.

Policy analysis needs good descriptions of what is happening. In complex situations, the different strands have to be disentangled, and this usually calls for some theoretical appraisal of relationships and issues. But that appraisal does not depend on an explanation of mechanisms – or *why* things happen – at all. That is true, in part, because we do not need to understand mechanisms to anticipate outcomes. More fundamentally, it is true because the way into a problem is not necessarily the way out of it. If you fall down a deep hole, an understanding of the principle of gravity is not going to help you very much. It helps to take stock of the situation, to know where you are and what resources you have to hand. What you really need to know, however, is how to climb out. In the case of poverty, the most successful measures against poverty have probably been economic growth,[170] the development of social protection systems[171] and the empowerment of the poor.[172] They have all grown out of practice. None of them has depended on a causal analysis, or on an understanding of the reasons for poverty.

The main alternative to the rationalist model is incrementalist and pragmatic: the best method is the one that happens to work in context, not necessarily the one that makes most sense. Edmund Burke recommends this approach as the most practical route to sound government:

> By a slow but well-sustained progress, the effect of each step is watched; the good or ill success of the first, gives light to us in the second; and so, from light to light, we are conducted with safety through the whole series. We see, that the parts of the system do not clash. The evils latent in the most promising contrivances are provided for as they arise. One advantage is as little possible sacrificed to another. We compensate, we reconcile, we balance.[173]

When things only work in part, the best route is often to focus on small-scale, piecemeal improvement, building on the strengths rather than dwelling on the weaknesses. The key is to refine, modify, and adjust methods as things happen, testing the effects rather than refining the theory. In the construction of policy overall, incrementalism can be confusing, muddled and aimless. In the selection of methods, by contrast, it is practical, modest in its claims to knowledge, and open to experience. This is the area where incrementalism really comes into its own.

Exercise

Review government policy on any aspect of social exclusion (www.seu.gov.uk), such as the regeneration of poor areas or the prevention of teenage pregnancy. What methods have been adopted? How can it be established whether such methods are effective? What other methods might be used?

EIGHT

Selecting methods: value for money

The central issue in selecting methods is effectiveness – the extent to which a method achieves the aims of the policy. However, there are other important issues to consider, and when policy makers are considering what the best options are, new criteria tend to be applied – issues like cost, practicality and how the policy will be interpreted publicly. Just which method is adopted has to depend on the specific circumstances.

Effectiveness, efficiency and value for money

The main test of policy is to ask whether it meets its objectives. This is 'effectiveness'. In real life, however, effectiveness is rarely pursued at the expense of every other consideration. The selection of methods depends not just on whether something works, but how it works when the costs are taken into account, and whether the return is proportionate to the effort. This is often summed up in terms of 'value for money'. 'Best value', for example, placed a duty on local authorities and some other agencies

> to make arrangements to secure continuous improvement
> in the ways its functions are exercised having regard to a
> combination of economy, efficiency and effectiveness.[174]

The issues of economy, effectiveness and efficiency are the main subject of the first part of this chapter. The issues are financial ones, but 'finance' goes rather beyond the narrow sense of accountancy which it is usually associated with – and accountants are increasingly being asked to do the sort of work which is part of the training of a policy analyst. The kinds of question which are asked about 'value for money' are not just about money; they are also about value.

Costs

There are three key ways of understanding costs. The first, 'common-sense' approach is to look at costs as an 'average' – that is, the mean for each item, derived by adding up the sum of all costs and dividing it by the number of items. The Office of the Scottish Ombudsman has been reported as costing £2,727,000 per annum;[175] in 2004-05 it dealt with 2,377 enquiries.[176] On that basis, processing each enquiry costs about £1,150. (This is oversimplified, because it puts aside ancillary work like outreach, liaison and other work for the promotion of standards; nor does it consider the costs of each enquiry to the agency under investigation. Dealing with enquiries is the Ombudsman's primary mode of operation, however, so it still serves as a useful indicator.)

The second approach is to review the marginal cost – the cost of adding further items. If an agency has spare capacity, dealing with extra enquiries will bring down the average cost. Because many of its costs are already committed, like salaries and accommodation, it may be able to do the extra work with very little extra money. If the Ombudsman's office, which is still fairly newly established, was to deal with 600 more enquiries within its existing staff complement, the marginal cost would mainly be the cost of the enquiry itself, such as communication and travel, and it should bring down the average cost of an enquiry to less than £1,000. If, by contrast, each extra enquiry demands more staff time, at the current average of about 60 cases per member of staff per year, appointing 10 more members of staff may require more office space and consequently cost much more.

For practical purposes, many of the decisions which need to be made are about changing direction rather than the existence of the organisation, and marginal costs are consequently much more likely to be important than average costs.

An idealised production function is shown in Figure 8.1. As production increases, average costs tend to fall slowly, then start to rise. Marginal costs tend to be below average costs when production is limited, but they rise rapidly when obstacles are reached.

The third type of cost is the economic concept of 'opportunity cost'. This is the cost of not doing something else with the money. This does not appear in balance sheets, and it is much more difficult to assess, but it is part of any sound appraisal of the costs and benefits of undertaking different programmes.

Cost-effectiveness

A policy is effective if it meets its aims. It is cost-effective if it meets its aims at the lowest price possible. This is not the same as saying that it is cheap, because cheapness can often only be achieved by compromising the objectives. Further, as the previous section suggests,

Figure 8.1: An idealised production function

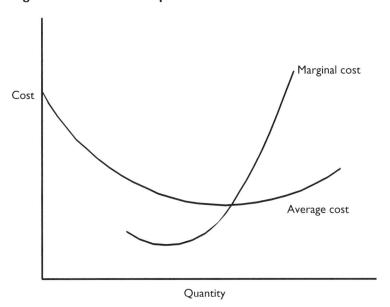

what is counted as a 'cost' is not straightforward. Costs can include average costs, marginal costs or opportunity costs. Cost-effectiveness is likely, then, to be open to discussion.

Discussions of cost-effectiveness tend to focus more on costs than on effectiveness. Saying that a policy is cost-effective is not a judgment about whether it was worth doing in the first place; it is saying that the aims have been achieved at the minimum cost. More commonly, cost-effectiveness is assessed in relative terms. If two methods yield the same results – or at least, if there is not much to choose between them – the cheaper method is the one to go for. This is the basis of *cost-effectiveness analysis*, or CEA. CEA works by comparing the relative costs and effectiveness of alternative methods. A classic example compared the cost and effectiveness of two competing methods for dealing with varicose veins – surgical stockings or surgery. Both had similar results, but the surgical stockings were cheaper and involved fewer risks.[177] CEA has been very widely used in health care.[178]

In welfare economics, preferences are expressed largely in terms of trade-offs – people tend to want more, but they will usually take less of one thing to get more of another. There are certainly trade-offs that policy makers do make, whether or not they admit to them. They may say that the value of life is beyond price; they may well mean it, especially if the life is their own; but when push comes to shove, there is a practical limit as to how much they are ready to spend in the attempt to keep someone else alive. In the NHS, there is an implicit limit to how much the service will spend for limited benefit – estimated, in 2002, as somewhere in the region of £30,000 for each 'quality-adjusted life year' gained through medical intervention. Alan Williams argues:

> Nature abhors a vacuum. These people have to make decisions and they will make the decisions. Out of their decisions, wittingly or unwittingly, there will come to be a pattern of activity.[179]

The main problems in assessing cost-effectiveness come from decisions about marginal costs – the cost of doing a little bit more. This leads us on to the related issue of 'efficiency'.

Efficiency

Efficiency is often confused with cost-effectiveness. A process is cost-effective if it meets its objectives at the lowest possible cost. It is efficient if produces goods or services at the lowest possible cost per unit. Sir Peter Gershon's report, *Releasing resources to the front line*[180] uses the term to refer to a range of cost-savings and increased outputs. The definitions include:

1. 'reduced numbers of inputs ... whilst maintaining the same level of service provision';
2. 'lower prices for ... resources';
3. 'additional outputs';
4. 'improved ratios of output per unit cost of input'; and
5. 'changing the balance between different outputs'.[181]

Most of these are examples of cost-effectiveness rather than efficiency. Gershon's first and second definitions are about cutting costs, or 'cost minimisation'. This may be part of efficiency or cost-effectiveness, but is not enough to guarantee either. The third is concerned with improved achievement of aims, which is probably about greater effectiveness – although it could also, arguably, be an example of pointlessly doing more. Only the last two definitions are about efficiency.

Although efficiency and cost-effectiveness sound very similar, they are quite different. The difference is most easily explained graphically. Figure 8.2 shows a model production function.

Figure 8.2: A model production function

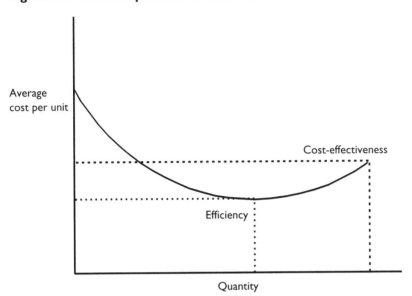

Efficiency is maximised at the bottom of the curve. The most cost-effective approach, by contrast, is found at the right-hand edge of the curve, where average costs are higher, but aims are achieved to the maximum degree.

Efficiency improves when the ratio of costs to outputs is improved. The 'cost-efficiency' targets of the NHS are intended to cut the unit costs of treating each patient. Cost-efficiency targets are based on reference costs for a range of NHS hospital activity. Unit costs are identified by taking the total number of costs and dividing that by the number of cases treated. Dawson and Jacobs explain: 'The only way to achieve an 'efficiency gain' is to increase the number of patients treated per pound of the budget'.[182] In the example considered earlier, the average cost per enquiry of the Ombudsman's office could be reduced by dealing with more enquiries, but it would take a very large number of extra cases to have a significant effect. A policy to bring down average costs substantially would need a much more radical rethink of the management system – decisions, for example, about business processes (for example, reception and filtering), triage (selection of significant cases), rationing (for example, the reduction of staff time spent on each case) or the allocation of resources (reviewing the staff complement). There is a combination here of cost reduction, productivity gains and reduction in service.

The prospect of reducing services is what really distinguishes efficiency from cost-effectiveness. Unit costs depend on how expensive each case is to deal with. Achieving every aim may be inefficient, because some aims are more expensive and difficult than others, and because costs are likely to rise when agencies are straining to meet targets. In the case of the Ombudsman, triage (reducing the response to cases that are less likely to make a difference) might be used to reduce average costs. In the NHS, where demand is much higher, triage has been used (for example, in initial sorting of primary care cases), but it might be more efficient to treat more less-problematic patients, and ignore the more problematic ones. In either case, there may be a trade-off between efficiency and cost-effectiveness.

In economic theory, productive efficiency is one of the results from competition, and attempts to introduce commercial factors, marketisation and competition into the public sector are generally concerned with efficiency in this sense. From the perspective of the public sector, however, achieving productive efficiency requires some compromise in service objectives. For example, adverse selection – refusing to deal with cases which are more difficult, or circumstances where needs are more severe – may improve the ratio, and so increase productive efficiency. Public services are often accused of being less efficient than private services. That is probably right. Public services are not supposed to be efficient. They are supposed to be cost-effective, which is something else entirely.

The other use of 'efficiency' in economics is allocative efficiency. Allocative efficiency occurs when the balance of production matches demand. Demand in economics is mainly understood in terms of individual preference, expressed through the mechanisms of the market. In public sector provision, however, 'demand' is mainly expressed in other ways – through the assessment of need, the exercise of choice, and user empowerment – and the interpretation of demand is strongly subject to social and political aims and values. For that reason, the idea of 'allocative efficiency' is not much used in this context.

Case study: Contracting out

One of the central differences between public and private provision has been the relative weight given to effectiveness, in the case of the public sector, and efficiency, in the case of the private sector. This has often been a matter of concern for those who wish the public sector to be more efficient.

In the private sector, contracting out services can be used to maximise efficiency. If a sub-contractor can provide a core service more cheaply than it can be done in-house, there is an argument either for focusing production on the areas where the business's return is the greatest, or for contracting the service out. (This is, at best, a rule of thumb. A restaurant usually makes more money from coffee and wine than it does from the food. However, it does not follow either that it should contract out the provision of food, or that it should stick to serving coffee.)

Applying the same principle to the public sector does not, however, mean that public sector provision would become efficient, or that it should be. The public sector is not meant to be efficient; it is meant to be cost-effective. The central argument for contracting out is that, under certain conditions, it can help to make the public sector more cost-effective. It does that by maximising efficiency at a series of intermediate stages. Figure 8.3 is based on work done for the Audit Commission. In community care, provision has to be made for several different levels of need, becoming progressively more expensive as more input is required. Drawing lots of production curves for providers should, in principle, make it possible for the commissioning body to maintain cost-effectiveness, while each provider is aiming for efficiency. The main flaw in this argument is that the shape of the production curve for the public sector does not stay the same when services are contracted out; it is affected by the costs of having to meet residual needs not otherwise provided for, and by issues like economies of scale. There is no guarantee, then, that having contracted out certain parts

Figure 8.3: Multiple providers

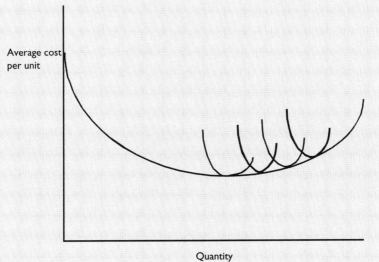

135

of the service, that cost-effectiveness can be maintained in the others. There may, too, be costs involved in contracting out – issues such as transaction costs, the costs of inspection and monitoring, and opportunity costs – which mean that the process becomes more expensive rather than less.

It is possible, in principle, for contracts to be done at arm's length, so that the provider is principally responsible for delivering specified results. In practice, however, there is a growing emphasis on securing contract compliance, often with highly detailed specifications of arrangements. These topics are dealt with in a standard service contract used by one Scottish local authority:[183]

- identification of the functions and objectives of the service;
- core values;
- the specific terms on which services will be provided, including geographical area, times of opening, and service location;
- details of staffing, including level and training;
- coordination with other services;
- record keeping; and
- engagement in quarterly monitoring and evaluation of contract compliance.

The Audit Commission has identified a range of problems associated with the purchasing role in health authorities. They include:

- the size of the task;
- the inadequacy of information about needs;
- poor organisational integration between those assessing needs and those responsible for purchasing;
- inadequate measures of effectiveness;
- different amounts spent on the contracting process;
- over-use of block contracts, leading to inflexibility;
- reliance on fixed prices, which do not reflect variations in the levels of work done;
- over-specification of quality, which is unenforceable; and
- unpredictable timing in the negotiation of contracts, which leads to uncertainty about pricing.[184]

The implication of these criticisms is that purchasing authorities may over-reach themselves: the attempt to secure the minutiae of contract compliance may make the contracts unenforceable in practice.

Cost-benefit analysis

A standard means of determining the appropriateness of a policy is to establish whether it offers sufficient benefits to outweigh its costs. The basic technique is called *cost-benefit analysis*, or CBA. CBA requires all costs, and all benefits, to be taken into account.

This approach is beset with problems. Much of the literature is concerned with technical issues. The technical problems include:

- identifying the nature of costs (as considered before);
- identifying what constitutes a benefit (on the same basis);
- allowing for inflation, or changes in the value of money;
- discounting for the future. The further away the benefits are, the more uncertain they become. Many capital projects are built for a 30-year life or beyond; it is conventional gradually to discount future values by taking off a proportion of costs. The Treasury's *Green book* recommends a discount rate of 3.5% per annum. At that rate, £1,000 now is worth £709 in 10 years' time;[185]
- the valuation of intangibles, such as a person's time, or the value of life. Time is a key element in the determination of the benefits of transport projects. A person's life has to be valued because people are likely to be killed in major construction projects. A modified version of CBA is *planning balance sheet analysis*, which puts costs and benefits into columns while leaving intangibles unquantified.

There are also two key issues of principle. The first issue concerns distribution: those who pay are not necessarily those who benefit. Technically, CBA assumes that the winners could benefit the losers (the 'Hicks-Kaldor' criterion[186]); but this is not the same as saying that they will actually do so. The second issue concerns the use of money as the basis of valuation. Cash values are taken as given, but cash values can reflect questionable standards. In cash terms, a house which is worth £300,000 is worth six times a group of five flats each worth £50,000. That means that given the choice between putting a road across the site of a £300,000 house occupied by one household, or a block of low-priced flats occupied by five households, it is the flats which will be knocked down.

By comparison with CBA, cost-effectiveness analysis – which was referred to earlier – is a modest, limited application of the same techniques. Because the aims are given and tightly defined, CEA is mainly focused on costs, and the trade-off between costs and outcomes is made explicit. Because effectiveness is defined by the aims of the policy, CEA makes it possible to ignore some of the intangibles, which are the same for each of the competing methods.

CBA and its variants get extensive coverage in the literature. Partly, this is because it is one of the very few applied methods that Economics has given to the world, and economists have made a lot of it; partly because it is a useful illustration of general principles. There are some classic examples where CBA has been used. One is the case made to put prescription medicines in child-proof containers, where it was argued, persuasively, that the total cost would amount to only £20,000 for each child's life saved.[187] But the attempt to extend CBA to other applications has been much less convincing. Consider, for example, the bizarre case of the CBA for the treatment of syphilis.[188] The central question put in Klarman's study is whether it is worth treating venereal disease at public expense. The outcome of the CBA hangs on the value of the shame or stigma experienced by unfortunate sufferers.

The truth is that CBA, in the unvarnished form it appears in economics textbooks, has only a limited application in practice. Even in health care, where there is now an extensive literature, the use of the materials is treated with some scepticism. Reinhardt complains:

> Policy-makers worldwide are on a quest to control national spending for health care and to enhance the value received for whatever is being spent on health care. One should think that the economic evaluation of clinical practice would play a major role in this quest. Alas, so far it has not ... few key decision-makers anywhere in the industrialized world seem to rely on these types of analysis in their daily operations.[189]

In the UK, some problems, like road-building, have lent themselves to the process, and CBA is fairly routine in major construction projects. By contrast, in relation to most social policy, CBA is rarely applied. This is because CBA has little to say about the distributive implications of policy, and distributive issues are fundamental to social policy.

Distributive issues

Equity, the principle of 'equity' or fairness is an important issue in service delivery. Equity means that like cases are treated alike. Where there are differences, those differences are reflected in differences of treatment; where there are none, distinctions between cases are unfair and arbitrary. Procedural fairness is concerned with procedures, like non-discrimination; substantive fairness with outcomes. Le Grand points to several different measures of outcomes relevant to equity:

- *public expenditure* – whether people have different amounts of money spent on them;
- *final income* – whether the amount of money spent has an equivalent effect on the recipients;
- *use* – whether people are able to use the service to an equivalent extent;
- *cost* – whether people suffer equivalent costs as a result of their problems; and
- *outcome* – whether people finish in equivalent positions.[190]

The term 'targeting' can be used for any attempt to identify a client group. Policies may be focused on a range of different groups: individuals, households, families, communities, areas and sections of the population. Policies which apply equally to everyone are exceptional – most 'universal' benefits are, in fact, categorical, and targeted at a broad class of people in need (like children or old people) as a way of addressing needs within the group.

The language of 'targeting' is sometimes muddled with other issues, especially selectivity (measures to exclude people who should not be affected) and means testing.[191] Targeting does not need to do either: for example, a soup kitchen does not have to be means tested, and it does not have to turn people away, but it is clearly targeted. There are policies which are not targeted at all, like public service broadcasting, but many which seem not to be targeted, like libraries or advice centres, actually have a geographical focus, and others, like helplines or websites, have implicit biases to people who are able to gain information about them and access them. Most public policies are intended to have an effect, and to have an effect on someone – a group of people, people in a certain area, people with particular needs, or the like. The effectiveness of the policy depends on whether or not the target population is reached.

The central arguments for targeting are arguments for equity and efficiency. Targeting is equitable if it directs resources to people who ought to have them and denies them to those who should not. It is efficient if it yields the greatest benefit for the target group at the least possible cost, wasting as little as possible. Three main problems can reduce efficiency:

- *deadweight* – people receive the service or benefit, but their circumstances are not materially affected by the measure;

- *spillovers* – people are helped who it was not intended or necessary to help;
- *low take-up* – there is failure to reach those at whom the policy was targeted.

Effectiveness – whether a policy achieves its aims – is compromised mainly by the third problem, low take-up. Although the first two affect efficiency (how much a policy costs, and how much is wasted), they do not necessarily mean that the policy is failing.

Redistribution, any policy is redistributive if the person who receives a benefit is not the same as the person who pays. That much is true of every public service. 'Vertical' redistribution takes place between richer and poorer people. A policy is said to be 'progressive' when it transfers resources from rich to poor, 'regressive' when it redistributes from poor to rich, and 'proportionate' or 'neutral' when it does neither. Subsidies to primary schooling, for example, are progressive, because young families tend to be poorer; subsidies to university education are regressive, because older families are less poor, and the selection of university students is overwhelmingly biased to the higher social classes. Table 8.1 comes from work by Glen Bramley, reviewing the distributive implications of local government expenditure in the UK.[192]

'Horizontal' redistribution takes place when transfers are made between categories of people, irrespective of income. Social insurance pensions are not based in savings; they are a transfer from workers to older people. Statutory maternity pay transfers money from men to women, from non-employed people to workers, from people without children to people with children.

The Treasury's *Green Book* recommends that people appraising policy should consider the distributive impact of policy, and that where they do not do so, they should justify that position.[193]

Table 8.1: The distributive effects of local services

Strongly for the better off	Moderately for the better off	Neutral or ambiguous	Moderately pro-poor	Strongly poorer
Higher education	Waste tips	*Neutral:*	Social care for older people:	Social housing
Education 16-19	Car parks	Secondary schools	day care	Housing advice
Adult education	Markets	Mental illness	meals	Welfare rights
Car and road users	Libraries	Playgrounds	home care	Social services for children
	Museums	Environmental services	Buses	
	Sports	*Ambiguous:*	Bus passes	
	Swimming	Nursery schools	Community centres	
	Arts	School meals	Primary education	
	Entertainments	Careers	Further education	
		Youth services	Special education	
		Special transport	Community regeneration	
		Consumer advice	Services for disabled people	

Source: G Bramley, G Smart, 1993, *Who benefits from local services?*, London: STICERD, London School of Economics and Political Science. Reproduced with permission from Glen Bramley.

Case study: The Poll Tax

This is a cautionary tale. The Community Charge, or 'Poll Tax', was one of the most notable disasters of public administration in the last 30 years. It has several competitors – the same government presided over a series of administrative bungles, including Housing Benefit (1982), Child Support (1991) and Incapacity Benefit (1995) – but none of the others led to riots in the streets.

Before the introduction of the Community Charge, local government was paid for mainly through a combination of central government funding and domestic rates. Rates were a tax levied on the notional rental value of property – very much a 'notional' value, because the valuation of property was not related either to income or to property values. People with no other income received benefit payments to cover the costs of rates; in 1967, the Labour government introduced 'Rate Rebate', a means-tested benefit for people on low incomes. This was unified, in 1982/83, with the system of Housing Benefit.

The main arguments for rates were that property taxes would discourage under-occupation and that they were roughly associated with resources. The main arguments against were that they were not well related to income, costing more, for example, for pensioners occupying large housing than for working families. In poorer areas, the burden of rates was spread across lower value properties, meaning that rates tended to be high in the areas least able to afford them. (This is a problem with all local taxation.)

The proposal for a Community Charge was intended to change the basis of taxation from property to persons. Every person aged 18 or over resident in an area would become liable to the Community Charge. This would mean that residents with no responsibility for property would also become liable. Further, the government determined that the benefit regime would be altered, so that even the poorest people would have to pay some proportion (generally 20%) of the Community Charge. This, on the face of the matter, was massively regressive. It would reduce the liability of richer people, while increasing the liability of poorer people.

The Green Paper proposing the Community Charge, however, claimed that the policy would be distributively neutral, and even favorable to people on low incomes. Poorer households tend to be smaller than richer households; households with adult children tend to have more earners on higher salaries than others. The document claimed:

> at the lowest income levels, householders would face lower average bills with a full community charge than with domestic rates. Overall a community charge would perform no worse than the rates.[194]

This statement depended on three principal assumptions: the vertical nature of the redistribution, the numbers of adults in low-income households and the availability of Community Charge rebate. Each of these assumptions was flawed. The first assumption is the one that should have been picked up: there were going to be winners and losers. The Green Paper recognised:

> The move from rates to a community charge will inevitably affect the personal finances of households since single-adult households gain at the expense of multi-adult households.[195]

The Poll Tax did not only shift liabilities from poor to rich. It had a horizontal impact, transferring liabilities from some low-income households (for example, single pensioners) to other poor households (for example, young people in houses in multiple occupation), and from householders to non-householders. The main losers were expected to be 'other single adults'.[196]

In relation to the second, the trend was more difficult to spot at the time: the numbers of adults in richer and poorer households were changing. Ten years before, the largest sector of poor people were pensioners; 10 years later, they were younger families with children. This meant that households with two adults on low incomes could indeed face higher bills than households on higher incomes with one. The third assumption was subject to the predictable problem that take-up of benefits was low.

The problems that sank the Community Charge were not, however, problems of distribution. The distributive issues did lead to a widespread perception of unfairness, which legitimised protests and fuelled civil disobedience. Two other issues, however, were probably more important. One of the key problems was that the level of Community Charge was much greater than foreseen. At the same time as it was trying to introduce the Community Charge, the government was reducing the Exchequer contribution to local authorities. If two thirds comes from central government, and one third from local taxation, the effect of withdrawing 1% of support is to increase the local contribution by 2%. If central government had maintained previous levels of contribution, the Community Charge might have been set at a quarter of its actual cost – a figure which almost certainly would have had an effect on the levels of compliance. The final, core weakness of the idea of the Community Charge was administrative. The pilot in Scotland showed that people moved far more often than registrars had thought. Pursuing people for payment proved highly problematic. The Green Paper considered operational problems in an appendix[197] and opined that: 'These problems are not insuperable'.[198] They were.

Exercise

What are the distributive implications of altering pension ages?

NINE

Analysing implementation

In an ideal world, what an administration might be expected to do is what the agency is directed to do. Policy goes in at the top, and a service delivery comes out at the bottom. This is the model of 'perfect administration'. Perfect administration is an ideal type, rather than a realistic expectation. It is commonly associated with a bureaucratic model, where rules are made centrally and the operation of the service follows an undeviating chain of command from top to bottom. (This idea is often attributed to Weber – Haralambos, for example, suggests that bureaucracy, to Weber, is 'rational action in an institutional form'[199] – although Weber's work on rational administration is actually rather more sophisticated.[200]) It is important to realise that there are discrepancies between the aim and the process: if we wanted 'perfect administration', bureaucracy would not be the way to do it. Perfect administration calls for a command structure, like the structure of an army. In an ideal army, each person works as part of a unit. There is a surrender of individual decision making and submission to higher authority in all things. In a bureaucracy, by contrast, each person has a defined role and set of tasks, makes decisions in their sphere of influence, and is accountable to the next person above them. In the army, if no-one issues instructions, nothing happens, unless someone assumes command. In a bureaucracy, if no-one issues instructions, every member of the bureaucracy knows exactly what to do – which, incidentally, is why local government departments can survive without anyone apparently being in charge for months or years. In the ideal army, there is a chain of command: a major in the army can instruct a private. In a bureaucracy, there is a chain of accountability: the director of a local government department does not issue orders to the typists. (For what it is worth, the British army is much more like a bureaucracy than an idealised command structure: officers are responsible for strategy, but sergeants manage the troops.) Equally, in the other kinds of decision making and organisational structure outlined in Chapter Two, there are several alternative formal arrangements for arriving at decisions at intermediate levels of the process.

There are many different ways of understanding and interpreting the process of implementation. For the purposes of this book, three main classes of explanation should be helpful: implementation as a structural process, as a political process, and as a policy process.

Implementation as a structural process. Every policy has to have some kind of administration, and where structures exist, they acquire their own rationale and methods of working. Services can be distinguished by:

- the functions of the organisation – education, social work, health, and so on;
- the client group the organisation serves – services for children, for elderly people, and so forth;
- the geographical area which is served.

Every administration has to find ways of operationalising policy – translating it into practice. The same issues which lead to divisions of labour between services also imply further divisions of labour within them. But the same divisions imply further issues of coordination, and more gaps between policy in theory and policy in practice.[201]

Some models of administration represent it as a process of learning; some as an incremental or experiential process, a sort of 'evolution'.[202] 'Evolution' means that things that work survive, and things that do not work have to be dropped. There are often adaptations to circumstances. An example is the development of 'service ideologies'. One of the key reasons why service ideologies develop is because officers are exposed to common pressures. Social workers are subject to pressure from inquiries, the courts and the media; it has fostered a general view that 'statutory responsibilities' and the management of risk, interpreted narrowly in terms of child care and court work, dominate the service agenda, even though the client load, financial pressure and balance of statutory responsibility actually seems to point social work services towards elderly people. Housing providers are most subject to pressure from service users and community organisations, which has led to a much greater emphasis within housing services on equity and procedural fairness than on risk assessment. At the same time, it would be unwise to assume that everything that is done is there because it is needed. Public sector organisations tend to be fairly conservative institutions, where people often assume that the way things are done is the obvious or only way to do them, and they are keen to leave well alone. A recurring mantra is, 'if it ain't broke, don't fix it' – a comment which can be relied to appear in almost any context, applying to organisational machines that are not just malfunctioning, but out of control and slicing up the office staff with rotating knives.

Implementation as a political process. Implementation can be seen as an arena where different factions, interest groups and approaches compete, deliberate and negotiate approaches. A lot of the literature on administration is written by political scientists, and perhaps unsurprisingly they tend to find political elements in every part of the structure. Some have described implementation in terms of coalitions of interests, some as a structure with a series of actors, some as a symbolic political process.[203] The idea of the 'rational', self-interested bureaucrat draws on economic modelling to predict outcomes; other models have emphasised different motivations in bureaucratic practice, including a belief that the service is making a contribution to society.[204] Any emphasis on the independent motivation of people in bureaucracies brings them squarely into this category.

Implementation as a policy process. Overlapping with both these views is the idea that implementation is a policy process in its own right. It has all the elements of policy making – a structure of decision making, the contribution of different actors, and the problems of translating policy into practice. Several approaches to implementation emphasise the 'perspective' of implementation, either treating implementation as a process, or reading backwards from outcomes to identify the motivations, process and effects. For practical purposes, it is difficult to avoid treating implementation in these terms. Implementation has to be seen both as a part of the policy process, and as a process in its own right, which has to be mapped and checked to work out what is happening in practice.

Understanding implementation

Most examinations of implementation start from the simple basic premise that the administration is not perfect. Perfect administration is a yardstick – the test of what ought to happen. Implementation is what actually does happen. Evaluations begin with the policy, look at the implementation, and identify how far the implementation is consistent with the policy. The problem with that approach is that there are many reasons apart from implementation why outcomes might differ from policy. The first task is to describe what is actually happening in the process of implementation.

There are three main approaches. The first is to begin with a theory of how the organisation works. Often this will be drawn from the formal statements of the organisation itself, or from previous studies of similar organisations; an example was given in Chapter Five, from

David Billis's work. When the organisation fails to conform to the ideal model, it might be because the model is wrong. Some inquiries into child abuse, for example, have assumed the procedures that ought to be followed, and taken the agencies to task when they did not apply those procedures. (It does not take much knowledge of the detailed process to anticipate what the reaction of people in the agencies is likely to be to that approach.) But it might also be true that the ideal model is right, and reality is wrong. One of the common features of scandals in institutional care is that indefensible practices become accepted as routine within the environments where they are used.

A second approach is to identify a series of stages within the process of implementation. This might involve examining illustrative cases, and checking what happens at each point along the route. A more aggressive approach from the management literature is 'business process engineering', which identifies the stages and proposes ways of shortening chains, circumventing problems or parcelling out parts of the operation. The principle in both cases is the same. Implementation is described as a sequential or linear process, and methods of dealing with policies or processes are tracked so as to find out what actually happens.

A third alternative is to examine implementation as a system. Systems analysis was introduced in Chapter Five. In this context, it calls for identification of a series of elements, or sub-systems, in the administrative process, and the identification of the relationships between them. This can be done in terms of sequential stages, but more usually a system will be a unit which is responsible for administering part of the process.

It can be difficult to try all these approaches, because when we deal with specific cases the options do not always make sense in context. For example, social work with families is not a uniform process, it is not sequential, and people who insist on model approaches (like one well-known lawyer who, chairing a child abuse inquiry, criticised the social workers in it for not reading the same paperback on child abuse that he had read[205]) are positively dangerous. Analysing social work processes in terms of systems is unfashionable, but it makes much more sense, and makes it possible to come to a range of different conclusions about the processes.[206] Administering pensions, by contrast, is a sequential process, and not one that has been subject to much theoretical analysis; it is a straightforward candidate for examination in stages, and it has indeed been the subject of 'business process engineering'.[207]

More rarely, there may be some circumstances where the choice between methods is not quite so obvious, and it is possible to do any (or all three) simultaneously. An example might be community care for elderly people. Looked at *sequentially*, the process would be to follow through the process as it affects an individual old person in a specific situation, such as discharge from hospital. The process might include: assessment and identification of needs; identification of options for service; selection of options; and service delivery.

Looked at as a *system*, the process would consist of:

- identification of actors – the old person, carers, social services, etc;
- the purchasing of services – social services management, budgeting and financial constraints, contracting with providers, etc; and
- the provision of services – the providers, the services offered, etc.

As a *theoretical model*, community care depends on the idea of welfare pluralism, or the 'mixed economy' of welfare. This points attention to:

- the sectors providing welfare – carers, statutory services, voluntary and independent providers;
- service planning and delivery through 'interweaving' packages of care; and
- coordination from the perspective of the individual service user.

In this case, there is no clearly 'right' way to look at the issues – any of them is plausible, and may be appropriate for different kinds of policy analysis.

Administration

Public administration is often stereotyped in particular modes. None of the stereotypes reflects practice everywhere, but they are often based in some common influences, and it is possible to identify some commonly recurring trends.

First, there are practical issues. Some key factors have a huge effect on the size, shape and pattern of the operation. They include:

- *Contact with the public.* Agencies which deal extensively and directly with the public have different needs for accommodation and personnel from those which do not. Personal contact affects access to buildings, reception areas, interview facilities, security arrangements and methods of recording. Extensive correspondence and the length of records have a major effect on information management. Where there are home visits, car parking for staff – always a vexed issue – becomes acutely important.

- *Accommodation.* Accommodation has a huge effect on management systems, staff relations and relations with the public. Some public agencies operate from converted houses on depressed estates; others work from purpose-built civic centres. Architects for public buildings often seem to pay more attention to a building's impact on the skyline, or the ability to defend buildings from rampaging villagers with pitchforks and firebrands, than they do to the impact of buildings on the services that occupy them. C Northcote Parkinson once suggested that the point where an agency got the perfect building was the point at which it tumbled into terminal decline.[208]

- *Information management.* The central test of information management is that it should be fit for purpose. Major problems have been caused for administrations which have ignored simple basic precepts and practices. The Child Support Agency compounded its early problems by failing to keep case files in alphabetical order. The Victoria Climbié inquiry, to take another example, comments that in one authority 'the case recording throughout was grossly inadequate and the likelihood of cases drifting or being lost was high',[209] while in another authority it commented on the 'haphazard and chaotic nature of the administrative system':

> Victoria managed, during the time that her case was open in Brent, to acquire five different 'unique' identification numbers on the various systems that were designed to ensure that the progress of her case was effectively monitored.[210]

Information management used to mean 'filing', and it was a major part of the floor space of public offices until the advent of computers. Times have changed: the computer has taken over everywhere. Computers have many virtues. They can perform repeated calculations rapidly and accurately; they allow cross-referencing and sharing of information; they have improved the presentation of documents immeasurably. But they also have vices. They do not handle correspondence well, and basing files on computers makes it necessary to hold files in more than one place. Centralised systems are vulnerable to crashes. Custom-designed programs are error-prone and difficult to maintain. Modern public offices (especially the DWP) have been blighted by the purpose-designed program, intended to offer comprehensive responses to impossibly complex personal circumstances.

After the practical constraints, there are the constraints imposed by policy decisions outside the agency. They include:

- *The level of funding.* Many public sector operations are done on a shoestring, reflecting widespread pressure to be accountable for the use of funds. This is not always the most economical way of doing things: public officials can find they are wasting time, which is expensive, because they have not been allowed to order in enough materials to keep their work going.
- *Peripheral activity.* The bulk of public funding in most agencies is devoted to the mainstream, or 'core', operations. However, temporary funding, often for three-year periods, is commonplace. The emphasis on evaluation and justifying the expenditure means that work with agencies on this sort of funding represents a disproportionate amount of the work that policy analysts are asked to do.
- *Relationships with service users.* It has become fashionable, in some public services, to refer to service users as 'customers', in the belief that the term can be used loosely to suggest that they will be treated with some respect. They are not really customers.[211] Customers, in a commercial setting, have a contingent contractual relationship with a business. It is contractual because it is based in voluntary agreement and exchange; it is contingent because either party can withdraw. Relationships between public services and service users are not necessarily contractual, or voluntary. Users can be prevented from withdrawing. Equally, agencies can be prevented from withdrawing, because they have statutory duties, or their users have rights. But if users and services are tied to each other, the pattern of service delivery, and the structure of the services, has to reflect that relationship. Some services, like social work, probation and the police, have to have mechanisms to track and chase uncooperative users. (The Probation Service has moved to referring to its users as 'offenders' instead of 'clients'.[212]) Other services, like education, have had to introduce formal mechanisms for the termination of

relationships, including the exclusion of children from schools and the withdrawal of children from formal education.

The third set of influences are the conventions of administrative practice. These include:

- *Accountability.* Public services in a democratic culture have to be able to explain what has been done, and why. This leads to a substantial emphasis on 'paper trails' – the ability to show in writing what has been done, when and by whom.
- *The conventional patterns of public service.* The British Civil Service has been based largely on the conventions of the most senior staff, the 'First Division'. Those conventions include:
  - the view that actions of the Civil Service are taken in the name of the minister. In many local authorities, it is still common practice for letters to be signed in the name of the Director of Service, not the name of the person writing the response;
  - the guarantee of anonymity given to every officer making decisions. This does not apply in local authorities but does apply in central government agencies like the DWP;
  - an emphasis on confidentiality. (This has recently been made subject to Freedom of Information legislation, but is still strong in many services, especially the NHS – in areas going well beyond medical confidentiality.)

    Although these approaches have their origins in the highest levels of the service, they have been very widely applied: the administration of social security has generally depended on the application of similar rules, including for example the requirement that social security officers (and some people visiting social security offices) sign the Official Secrets Act.
- *Accounting practice.* The public sector works to some common financial standards. Typically in the UK this includes:
  - programme budgeting on an annual basis. Although central government has now introduced 'accruals accounting', which is more flexible, public sector agencies still have very limited ability to save or transfer money between years or between budget heads;
  - accounting for gross expenditure and income. All income is reported without deducting expenditure, and income which is earned cannot be used to offset expenditure;
  - preserving 'audit trails' through meticulous recording of petty expenses.

- *Service ideologies.* This has been explained before: different services have different accepted norms of conduct, the 'common sense' of the field of activity.
- *Ethical rules.* It is not legitimate to use the power which stems from a role in public service for personal gain – an example is taking a bribe, or payment from an agency. But the borderlines are fuzzy; if they were not, it would not be so easy for officers to fall foul of them. There are different, and potentially conflicting, models of conduct. What, for example, is expected of a public service worker who has been offered the opportunity to combine work for the agency with an independent consultancy? Within the bureaucratic model, this would generally be unacceptable, because the role of each person has to be understood in the context of the role within the organisation. Within the management model, this is often encouraged as completing the range and diversity of actions within the agency, and the agency would expect to participate in the work. Within the professional model, the issue is a matter for the individual, and subject to the professional's judgment about meeting other responsibilities.

Equally, some codes are dependent on the settings where they take place. An example of this is a rule of confidentiality. Confidentiality applies fairly strictly in the medical profession, but that has led to conflict with the bureaucratic structures of hospitals. (Currently the legal position is that notes made within a hospital belong to the hospital, not to the doctor.) In some settings, confidentiality is qualified: a social worker in criminal justice, for example, is an officer of the court, and has a duty to disclose material to the court (at the risk of being held in contempt) which overrides professional discretion. Confidentiality does not apply within bureaucratic structures, because a report to one person is a report to the whole agency: a failure to record, report and share information appropriately may be a legitimate ground of criticism. Identifying ethical issues, then, is often problematic.

The generalisations made in this section are largely defensible, but they need to be treated with caution. Patterns of administration vary between services, and even to some extent between offices. Very few general observations apply consistently. A policy analyst, materialising for the first time in a strange agency, cannot rely wholly on previous experience or book knowledge to decipher the codes of the organisation. There should be a paper trail somewhere, but even well-laid trails can be difficult to make sense of if implicit assumptions have not been made clear. Interpretation calls for an anthropological approach – talking, observing, and getting a feel for the culture.

Case study: Social housing allocation

Housing allocations are intended in principle to determine who should have priority for social housing properties, as and when the properties become available. People apply on a housing list or register, their circumstances are recorded, and they are ranked in order of priority. Because people cannot share the allocated properties, there are no equal priorities; there must always be some way of ranking one person above another. In most of the documents produced by housing organisations, allocations are presented in terms of one of four types of policy:

- 'points' schemes, which give priority according to a set of priorities;
- 'date order' schemes, where people are treated on the basis of 'first-come, first served';
- 'merit' schemes, where cases are treated 'on their merits'; and
- 'group' schemes, where a range of categories are treated by different rules.

This classification is very misleading. There are actually five main stages in the process of allocations:[213]

1. *Access to the housing list.* Prospective tenants have to identify themselves, and they have to be accepted onto the list before their application can be dealt with.
2. *Determination of categories of applicant.* People who have applied for rehousing are placed into categories, mainly according to the location and size of property available. People who want four-bedroomed houses are not considered to be in competition with single people looking for flats. Most social landlords run a large number of different lists.
3. *Identification of priority groups.* Some categories of people have a special status and are treated differently from others on the list – for example, homeless people, people with special medical needs or resident staff. Every scheme is a 'group scheme' to some extent.
4. *Assessment of priority within groups.* Once the groups are established, it has to be decided which person has the greatest priority. This is commonly done by 'date order', 'merit' or 'points schemes'. Date order has been shown to have serious disadvantages – the people who are most able to wait are generally those in less need – and the general trend in recent times has been to try to avoid the sense that this is a 'queue'.

5. *Matching of applicants with available property*. Even if a particular case appears to have priority, the process of matching individual people to particular properties commonly involves some further considerations. The considerations most often taken into account are the choices and preferences of applicants and the need to balance other management considerations.

The pattern of housing allocations has developed to deal with a range of practical constraints. I have mentioned one before, the size and location of properties. But there are several others, which can be just as important.

The management of the housing stock. Allocations are more a means of finding tenants for existing property than a way of finding property for people. Early research on allocations found that irrespective of what allocations policies said, the people who were likely to be housed were those whose households were the right size for two- or three-bedroomed houses: the ones who waited longest were people who wanted smaller or larger properties than that.[214]

Most social housing in the UK is good housing, but many of the properties available to let are defective. Suppose, for example, that a landlord has 3,000 good properties, and 200 socially undesirable properties. In a typical year, there will be 4% vacancies in the good properties, or 120 vacancies, and 20% vacancies in the undesirable properties, or 40. Each of the undesirable properties will be offered to three people; each of the desirable properties will go immediately. That means that there will be as many offers going on 200 undesirable properties as on 3,000 desirable ones. It also means that landlords have to find tenants desperate enough to accept the least desirable housing. Usually these will be people with no choice – people who are homeless, and people who are disadvantaged.

Fairness. Housing allocation is highly contentious, and often politicised. (It has largely been forgotten, but the flashpoint for the civil rights marches and troubles in Northern Ireland was discrimination in housing allocation.) The best defences for harassed officials are open transparent procedures, following strict published rules.

Response to public pressure. The pressures are huge. The issues around dealing with members of the public, many of whom are desperate to improve their lives, are considerable. For decades, housing managers used unofficially to 'grade' applicants according to standards of cleanliness and the likelihood they would be well-behaved as tenants: the practice allowed them to head off problems both from applicants who would be insulted by being offered 'bad areas' and from existing residents who would object to them rehousing the wrong type in their area. This does not happen any more – at least, as far as official policies go. But there may still be restrictions on people believed to be liable to anti-social behaviour, criminal activity or rent arrears.

Public housing provision is, perhaps to a surprising extent, a sort of 'market'. In the market, people who are more able to exercise choice are better able to command resources. In systems where some people are able to wait, to bargain, to negotiate, those people are able to get better housing. People who are not able to negotiate – people in precarious situations, people with few rights, and those who are desperate – get the worst housing. [215]

Process evaluation

Implementation tends to be a seen as a means to an end; the main test of whether implementation is successful is whether it produces the desired outcome. There are times when implementation itself is the outcome that matters – in health care, which is a form of social protection, it may matter more to people that they are treated civilly, promptly and responsibly than that they are cured.[216] These issues are, legitimately, the subject of analysis in their own right. Many policy analyses, however, are not concerned with outcomes. They take place at a time when a policy or project is starting out, is beginning to engage with issues, and some initial judgment needs to be made about whether the process is working. It is necessary, then, to have some criteria by which implementation processes can be judged *as processes*, rather than dealing with the more obvious question of whether they work. This is sometimes called a 'process evaluation'.

Calnan and Ferlie distinguish process analysis – evaluating what a process achieves – and process evaluation, which is understanding how it goes about things.[217] Many of the tests of process discussed in the literature – issues like coverage, reproducibility or how people react to a process[218] – are part of process analysis rather than process evaluation. If we focus solely on how processes work, it seems to me that there are three main criteria. They are:

- *consistency*, or integrity – whether the pattern of implementation is appropriate to the task which has been set;
- *conformity* – whether the process of implementation meets the standards and criteria appropriate to this kind of work; and

- *coordination* – whether the process being undertaken stands in appropriate relation to the work which is being done around it.

Consistency. Implementation procedures have to be fit for purpose. In the first place, they need to be consistent with the aims, values and goals associated with the policy. Structures for implementation can have different objectives from the objectives of policy – there is no inconsistency, for example, in commissioning a private-sector, profit-making organisation to deliver residential care for elderly people. Procedures should not, however, have objectives which are directly contradictory to the aims of the policy. There is a potential inconsistency in developing policies concerned with democratic participation and empowerment through a structure that is strictly hierarchical and unresponsive to user concerns; many local authorities, aware of that inconsistency, have substantially altered their approaches to planning, housing and social care.

Second, they have to be capable of delivering the method which has been determined. Stoker points to a range of problems brought about by the implementation of 'new public management': they include fragmentation of services, over-commitment (where the main effect of initiatives is to exhaust resources without making an impact) and 'goal displacement', where the initial objectives of policy are subverted by the techniques which have been employed to pursue them.[219]

In principle, the pattern of implementation that is being pursued should be chosen to fit the policy. Existing services are delivered through a range of models – Chapter Two introduced bureaucratic, professional, management and agency approaches. Different models are arguably appropriate to different tasks. The bureaucratic model in social security was developed to give uniform, predictable responses; the professional model in the NHS was intended to permit flexible, individuated, personal responses; management models have been used to offer efficient production geared to defined agency tasks. Conversely, some models are not really appropriate to certain circumstances: agency-based services are not really equipped to offer comprehensive services, professional services are not good at uniformity, bureaucracies are not good at flexibility, and management-based services are not geared to individual rights. But the kind of model that can be used in a service area is usually determined before the policy is decided. If a government wants to deliver a service that falls in the general category of medical care, that service generally has to be delivered within the existing structure of services. Immunisation, for example, gets delivered in the UK through general medical practices – a uniform service being delivered through a professional mechanism. This is not necessarily the best approach, and there is nothing self-evident about that arrangement – it used also to be delivered through schools – but the character of the institutional arrangements in place greatly limits the scope for different patterns of implementation.

Conformity. Because policy is implemented through a range of possible structures, there is no simple rule which can be applied in every case to say that something is being administered appropriately. Many services are not functioning on a bureaucratic model, and the standards that are conformed to are not necessarily the objectives of the policy. Typically there are three types of standards which are applied, all at the same time:

- criteria which apply to someone in a specific role (manager, planner, officer, and so on);
- standards which apply generally to professions or semi-professions (social work, medicine, education, policing, and so on); and
- standards which obtain in the agency (local government, charities, membership agencies, and so on).

Evaluating the process usually involves some external reference to standards, including professional codes, or comparisons with the operation of similar agencies elsewhere.

Case study: Identifying institutional racism

The idea of 'institutional racism' has been attributed to Stokely Carmichael, who used it to refer generally to a widely-held, systemic presence of racism in society.[220] In the UK, although the term has been used to refer to systemic racism in British society,[221] it has come to be used in the narrower, more closely focused sense of racism expressed in the actions of institutions. The Stephen Lawrence Inquiry defined it as 'the collective failure of an organisation to provide an appropriate and professional service to people because of their colour, culture or ethnic origin'.[222] Similarly, the Institute for Race Relations has suggested that institutional racism 'covertly or overtly, resides in the policies, procedures, operations and culture of public or private institutions – reinforcing individual prejudices and being reinforced by them in turn'.[223] That focus makes it an appropriate case study for the consideration of implementation.

The Stephen Lawrence Inquiry (also called 'the Macpherson Report') focused on a boy who was murdered in a racist attack. Stephen was left to bleed to death. At the outset, police failed to do anything to save his life;

subsequently they failed to pursue or apprehend the murderers, or to obtain necessary evidence, while his parents were fobbed off. In the view of the inquiry, the failure of the police to respond appropriately was not attributable solely to racism on the part of officers; that racism was compounded by incompetence, insensitivity, poor management and patterns of conduct which acted to reinforce racial disadvantage.

Institutional racism can arise through in several ways. They include:

- overt or covert prejudice;
- direct discrimination;
- discriminatory processes;
- the production of disadvantage; and
- systemic disadvantage.

Prejudice. Expressions of prejudice are probably the easy things on this list to identify: a spoken quotation or a written comment can be sufficient. The Macpherson Report notes several examples of 'unwitting' racism, including 'insensitive and racist stereotypical behaviour' and 'the use of inappropriate and offensive language'.[224] This is described as 'unwitting' because the officers themselves were unable to see that what they were saying was prejudiced.[225]

Direct discrimination. Direct discrimination depends on both prejudicial intent and the translation of that intent into policy or practice. This is probably the most difficult issue to identify in practice; it can require a level of proof which is unlikely to be forthcoming or confirmed by the perpetrators. The Lawrence Inquiry gives several examples of discriminatory behaviour motivated by prejudice, including, for example, jumping to conclusions, failure to take statements and brushing complaints aside.

Discriminatory processes. A discriminatory process is one which, if practised generally, would have discriminatory effects. The main example of a discriminatory process in the Macpherson Report is the police's 'inadequate' treatment of racist incidents, which the Report suggests is the root cause of the under-reporting of such incidents.[226]

This has proved to be a difficult area to monitor in practice. Individual disadvantage can be evidence of a discriminatory process, but there are individual circumstances where some discrimination can be justified in specific contexts – for example, in the case of whether someone subject to religious dietary restrictions can work as a food taster. Disadvantage might be produced in aggregate, but it may reflect other issues besides the process itself (such as problems a minority group has in society). Judgments about processes have tended in consequence to be guided by assumptions about 'good practice'.[227] Unfortunately, the field of equal opportunities has been bedevilled with ill-informed approaches – like 'equal opportunities' interviews which impose common structures on job applicants (which is the reverse of equal opportunity, because only those who fit the preconceived structure will do well), or racial quotas, which provably act to limit the opportunities they are supposed to create,[228] and were consequently made illegal in the 1975 Race Relations Act, and yet which are still being advocated by those who ought to know better.[229]

The production of disadvantage. Demonstrating disadvantage is largely a matter of identifying outcomes. Criticisms of the police service's use of 'stop and search' are based on the differential outcomes, which show that the policy is used disproportionately against minority groups.[230] Often disadvantage may be assessed through 'ethnic monitoring', but judging outcomes in terms of statistical representation works badly for locations where minority groups are diffused (which is true of many of the places in Scotland where I work), or in small-scale operations. The most successful studies have been those which have looked intensively at problems, like the detailed studies undertaken by the Commission for Racial Equality,[231] or the Lawrence Inquiry itself.

Systemic disadvantage. Showing that disadvantage is systemic – that is, that it occurs throughout a system – can be shown if the disadvantage is the product of deliberate policy, if it is cumulative, or if it is recurrent. Deliberate disadvantage occurs where policy makes discriminatory distinctions. The Macpherson Report explicitly exonerates the Metropolitan Police of any suggestion of deliberate disadvantage, but argues that it is institutionally racist on other grounds.[232] Cumulative disadvantage arises where the effect of a series of smaller processes is to add up to substantial disadvantage. This has been consistently demonstrated in the allocation of council housing, where progressive filters reduce the prospects of rehousing for minority ethnic groups.[233] Recurrent disadvantage is disadvantage evidenced by repeated examples over periods over time, for example in police recruitment, use of 'stop and search', or the treatment of racial incidents.

Coordination. The issues of coordination are sometimes referred to as issues of 'joined-up' government. Traditional patterns of service delivery often present problems for coordination, and those problems need to be overcome. Wherever services interact, there are going to be boundary problems – points at which responsibility is disputed, where the liability for costs is uncertain, or where there are different approaches. There are three main types of problem:

- functional problems, where services have different purposes and priorities;
- geographical problems, where services serve overlapping geographical areas (and serve them all from different budgets);
- professional problems, where professional priorities are different (for example, housing officers emphasise equity, while social workers emphasise risk).

One of the clichés of coordination is that 'we're all trying to do the same things really'. Of course we're not. That is why we have different services doing different things. But there are issues where the differences between services become obstacles to doing things effectively, and coordination is necessary to identify and resolve disputes.

The most fundamental approach to coordination has been the establishment of a division of labour. Once a division of labour has been established, officials will work within it without conscious examination of the process. A strong example was the division of labour between hospital doctors and primary medical care.[234] Coordination mainly takes place by a system of referral and communication – not always successfully, but it is so much part of the established system that it is virtually taken for granted. Another was the distinction, introduced in 1948, between social assistance and welfare services. The reluctance of social workers to engage in financial matters has been modified in several ways, most directly in the operation of community care, but it is still basic to understanding the profession nearly 60 years later. There are several risks in establishing divisions of labour – there may be gaps, there may be overlaps, and there may be conflict at points where different agencies are attempting to do contradictory things. But the proper response to these is to review the division of labour, not to remove it altogether.

The movement away from traditional bureaucracies to agencies, multi-level governance and management models has meant that the issues of coordination have become particularly acute. The main alternative to the division of labour is *networking* – forming relationships, and trying from those relationships to negotiate and develop decisions about tasks. The division of labour begins with the task and assumes that relationships will follow; networking begins with relationships, and looks to establish a task once the relationships are in place. Examples are partnership working, joint planning, joint finance, liaison groups and working parties. Networking is the dominant model in much of the literature, even if it is not the main model in practice. That is because most conscious effort goes into the actions that people take positively, and the documentation that people produce generally refers to conscious attempts to introduce policy.

Many policy analyses are only concerned with parts of the whole, but there may be some point at which a policy analysis has to examine the process of partnership and networking. Because the process begins with relationships, the emphasis in the literature tends to fall on issues in relationships. Rhodes points to the importance of trust, interdependence and reciprocity;[235] Kearney et al to:

> a shared desire to work to common objectives, a high level of mutual trust, a willingness to cooperate, share responsibility, accept accountability, and where necessary to alter the prevailing administrative structures.[236]

But even if these conditions are desirable, and they provide a basis for recommendations for action, there is room for argument as to whether they are either necessary or sufficient for networks to work. The test of a partnership is not whether people feel good about each other; it is whether it adds value to the process. This may call for a review of the division of labour.

Networking and divisions of labour come together in certain fields, of which child protection is an important example. The problems of coordinating different professions came to the fore in the case of Maria Colwell.[237] Maria Colwell was a child who was abused and neglected by her stepfather after she had been returned to her mother from foster care. Although the inquiry has been seen as a criticism of social work practice, the report was more important as evidence of major deficiencies in the procedures for dealing with child abuse. A large number of workers had known something about the case – social worker, NSPCC officer, health visitor, GP, police officer, housing officer – but the information had never been collated. Since Colwell, the norm has been to appoint a 'key worker' to whom all information will be referred. The key worker is usually, although not always, a social worker. The functions of the key worker can be divided between *primary contact* and *role coordinator*. The primary contact is the worker most often seen by the family – perhaps a health visitor, probation officer or NSPCC officer – and role coordination may still be kept within social services, so that other workers (police officer, GP, housing officer, teachers) will refer to the right place. Despite the routine nature of these arrangements, continuing scandals reflect a common failure to implement them. The 2003 Green Paper comments:

> From past inquiries into the deaths of Maria Colwell and Jasmine Beckford, to recent cases such as Lauren Wright and Ainlee Walker, there are striking similarities which show some of the problems are of long standing. The common threads which led in each case to a failure to intervene early enough were poor coordination; a failure to share information; the absence of anyone with a strong sense of accountability; and frontline workers trying to cope with staff vacancies, poor management and a lack of effective training.[238]

The Green Paper proposes the development of an 'information hub' to ensure core access to key information for all agencies that need to know, the nomination of a 'lead professional', and work in multidisciplinary teams.[239] None of this is new – but, while the value of this sort of coordination is not disputed, it has not prevented previous failures.

The art of the possible

Politics, Bismarck famously said, is the art of the possible. Understanding implementation is fundamental to the success or failure of policies. Some of the issues about what is possible come into discussions about the identification of methods. Identifying constraints is part of determining which options are conceivable. Some of the issues belong in determining the selection of methods, because issues about implementation and administration affect the costs and benefits of different measures: the case study of the Poll Tax (presented in Chapter Eight) is about administration as well as being about distributive issues. And some of the issues belong here, because the analysis of the administrative process depends on identifying conflicts, contradictions between policy and method, and the ways in which the process of implementation channels and diverts policy from its intended course.

Keeping policy 'on track' is generally the remit of a programme or project manager. More generally, the tasks of determining how to implement new policy are considered, in public sector management, under the heading of 'managing change'. Policy analysis is an easier task than managing the process of change – a little like the difference between judging the speed of a tiger and riding on its back. Examining the process by which policy is implemented will benefit from some understanding of management, but the task is critical rather than experiential. The main tasks in examining processes are to find out what is going wrong, what could go wrong, and what might be done better.

What is going wrong. In principle, it should be possible to identify problems by a detailed audit and assessment of processes and the informed judgment of an expert analyst. But policy analysis is a political activity. It does not usually have much effect when analysts rely on their own arguments and reasoning to make a judgment about whether or not a policy is a good idea. There are some notable exceptions to that rule, such as the influential criticsms of the NHS made by Roy Griffiths[240] and Alain Enthoven[241], but those reports had their influence because they were commissioned to take a position in a favourable political environment. Effective criticism generally requires both evidence and support from within the commissioning organisation.

The most common technique for identifying what is going wrong is simply to ask people about it. Key actors and service users often have an acute sense of what is wrong with an organisation. There is a significant difference here in management practice in the private sector and the public sector. In the private sector, agencies which are underperforming have a strong tendency to put a favourable gloss on their performance. The way to attract resources and investment is to emphasise success; the price of failure is closure. In the public sector, by contrast, the opposite may be true. The way to argue for resources is to emphasise the deficiencies of the operation. Enoch Powell, a former Minister of Health, once wrote:

> One of the most striking features of the National Health Service is the continual, deafening chorus of complaint which rises day and night from every part of it, a chorus only interrupted when someone suggests that a different system altogether might be preferable.... The universal Exchequer financing of the service endows everyone providing as well as using it with a vested interest in denigrating it.[242]

Since the 1980s, the NHS has tried to restrain criticisms by threats against employees, and there are parts of the service where officials are reluctant to say much, but that approach has mixed success at best.

Provided that questions are framed in ways that make it possible to avoid interpersonal criticism and self-incrimination, it is still possible to draw out issues and concerns. (There is an example in the case study on referral processes, in Chapter Five. Health officials were asked to point to problems and deficiencies related to other services, rather than their own; the inquiry mined a rich seam of information.)

The main other standard way of assessing implementation is to use 'critical incidents' – case studies of issues where procedures have gone wrong.[243] Inquiries, inspections, audits and complaints can provide important insights into problems.

What could go wrong. There is a principle in engineering, sometimes called Murphy's Law, that 'anything that can go wrong will go wrong'. The reasoning behind the principle is that repeated iterations will find out any fault. If the odds of something going wrong are one in a million, and there are 10 million instances, it will probably go wrong 10 times. The same principle applies in public administration. Whenever human beings enter the consideration, which is difficult to avoid in most examples of public administration, someone, somewhere will gum up the works. The reason why residual systems for social security are so complicated is that people's lives are complicated, and no matter what contingencies have been anticipated, there will always be someone, somewhere, whose circumstances will not fit the existing rules.

Some of the techniques used to determine what might happen are the techniques of prediction, considered in Chapter Six. Some are arguments from analogy. Where there have been problems of a similar type in the past, those problems can happen again. Examples are the all-too predictable problems when protections against fraud are removed, when double-entry book-keeping is replaced by a new computer program, or when the frequency of inspections is reduced. The general understanding of 'good practice' in many fields reflects collective experience; it is not wise to disregard it.

One of the primary criteria used in analysis in this stage is not whether things will actually go wrong, but what the safeguards and alternatives are if they do. Many decisions taken in the public sector are dogged by uncertainty; it is not possible to be sure whether a policy will work, how it will work, or how the conditions around it will change. Sensible policies allow for the possibility that the policy makers may just conceivably be mistaken. The idea of 'robustness' was introduced in Chapter Seven, in the discussion of the operationalisation of methods: a robust decision is one which is capable of being changed, or which allows later options to be developed. Too often, policies are adopted with a wholly misplaced confidence in the quality of the analysis and the rightness of the solution. Allowing for uncertainty is not just a practical necessity; it is an ethical one.[244]

What might be done better. Recommendations for improvement are subject to much the same kinds of political constraint as findings of fault; they have the added disadvantage that, unless they have been piloted within a small part of the operation, they are rarely based directly in evidence from the organisation itself. The strongest arguments for adopting new practices are based on analogies with practice elsewhere – work done in similar agencies, or in response to similar constraints. This is one of the reasons why many agencies tend to imitate the practice of neighbouring agencies – there are often regional patterns in the delivery of local authority services like education, housing and personal social services. (Policy transfer tends to be reinforced by the exchange of personnel between neighbouring authorities, who bring related practice along with them.) Unless they are accepted and endorsed by the agency, recommendations are unlikely to be effective in practice.

Exercise

Is the NHS institutionally racist? Review the arguments in *The Department of Health Study of Black, Asian and Ethnic Minority Issues*, on www.dh.gov.uk, using the criteria considered in the case study on institutional racism.

TEN

The evaluation of policy

Evaluation has generated a literature, a set of disciplinary approaches and a specialised industry all its own. There is some overlap between evaluation and analysis for policy, and some of the books on evaluation talk about the subject in terms that could be read as books about policy analysis.[245] The focus of most guides to evaluation, however, falls on outcomes – they have relatively little to say about strategic planning, targets, indicators, forecasting, efficiency, robustness, the process of implementation, or indeed most of the other material covered up to this point.

In keeping with the general objectives of this book, this chapter is concerned with evaluation only in a limited sense. Policies are set in a particular context. They have aims. They select methods to implement those aims. They have effects. A basic policy analysis tests at each point whether each of the parts is consistent with the others. The most common pattern of evaluation in policy analysis is probably to check whether or not practice has been consistent with accepted guidelines, but a more fundamental, and often a more appropriate, approach is to see whether the outcomes of policy are consistent with the aims. In other words: has it done what it was supposed to do?

Summative and formative evaluation

Evaluation is commonly categorised in two main classes, summative and formative. *Summative* evaluation is the evaluation of a whole policy or process, focusing on the impact of policy. Most policy can be treated in terms of a series of categories – aims, methods, implementation and outcomes. A summative evaluation reviews each of the later categories to see whether or not the operation of policy is consistent with the aims. The impact of policy is mainly assessed by asking whether the policy has done what it set out to do. But summative evaluations may also take into account unintended consequences as well as the achievement of aims. Scriven distinguishes 'goal-based' and 'goal-free' evaluation.[246] 'Goal-based' evaluations ask only whether policies have met their goals. 'Goal-free' evaluations look at what policies are doing, rather than what they are supposed to do. A policy might be considered to be justified if it has had beneficial effects, even if the effects are not the effects that it was supposed to have. The distinction between goal-based and goal-free evaluation is picked up in the M*agenta Book*, the UK government guide to evaluation.[247] However, its understanding of goal-free evaluation is not the same as Scriven's: in the *Magenta Book*, a goal-free evaluation is one which looks at both intended and unintended consequences. This approach is not really 'goal free'; it still takes into account the aims of policy, along with other material which is additional to those aims.

Formative evaluation is undertaken at intermediate stages in the policy cycle. Formative evaluations can take place to see whether guidelines have been followed, to see whether an agency is ready to start work, to see whether an agency is being properly managed, or to see whether contract terms have been complied with. Typically this is done for peripheral projects and voluntary organisations, to see whether funding should be approved or continued. Properly speaking, this is an evaluation of part of the policy cycle, rather than the full evaluation of a policy in itself. Process evaluation, which I referred to in Chapter Nine, is a type of formative evaluation. The term implies a focus on the process, rather than on either policy or outcomes: that focus is inevitable if neither the policy nor the outcomes are subject to scrutiny.

The distinction between formative and summative evaluation is basically a technical one, concerned with the stage when evaluation takes place. Bate and Robert take the distinction a little further. People who think they are working on a 'summative' evaluation, they suggest, may be more inclined at the end of a process to believe that they are providing a final, authoritative answer, while those who think they are working 'formatively' may be more inclined to see it as part of an interactive work in progress.[248] The policy cycle, and rational policy making, lead back from evaluation into policy formation and development. In that sense, almost all evaluations are 'formative'.

Criteria for evaluation

Any evaluation has to be made in accordance with certain criteria, and the criteria need to be made explicit. Criteria for evaluation come from four main routes:

- they are specified by the agency which commissions the analysis;
- they are identified by the agency which is being evaluated;
- they are identified by stakeholders (such as partner agencies or service users) during the course of the evaluation; or
- they are attributed by the policy analyst.

The scope an analyst has for attributing criteria is limited. Policies are not evaluated on the basis that policy analysts like or dislike the original policy. No-one is terribly interested in hearing whether the policy analyst thinks that funding the agency is a good idea. No-one is going to welcome (or want to pay for) an evaluation that says 'no reasonable decision-making body could have thought that this policy was likely to work'. A notorious example was the Community Development Projects (CDPs) in the UK, which were set up to find ways to improve the problems of deprived urban areas. After several years of increasingly strident criticism, the CDP reports said that nothing worked, because the fault lay in the structure of capitalism. The exasperated government department closed them down.[249] The CDPs protested vigorously, but they had given the government every reason to get rid of them: if they were wrong they were not serving their purpose, and if they were right they were useless.

In practice, agencies are often vague about the criteria they want to apply, and the policy analyst may have to interpret their wishes for them. The sort of criteria I have applied under these circumstances include, in relation to internal process, accountability, transparency and robustness (the ability to cope with unexpected change); and, in relation to stakeholders and service users, community engagement, empowerment and responsiveness to need. Patton and Sawicki add a health warning, however: aims and criteria which are added only at the end of a process of review are often used as justifications of policy, rather than as genuine criteria. It is better to establish criteria early on.[250]

Case study: Audit

The idea of 'audit' owes its origins to financial scrutiny. It has gradually expanded, from an expanded focus on value for money, to cover a wide range of activities concerned with effectiveness, capacity, efficiency and probity.[251] The emphasis has shifted from policing to advice, guidance and support: 'the former guard dog', Martin writes, 'is retraining as a guide dog'.[252] The Audit Commission is responsible for auditing 'best value' agencies, including local authorities, the police and some transport agencies. Its local inspections mainly relate to activities in housing, environment and cultural activities. Social work and education are subject to different regimes, informed by professional criteria.

The Audit Commission describes its priorities as:
- assuring value for money and stewardship;

- measuring effectiveness;
- providing challenge and supporting change;
- focusing on service users and diverse communities;
- improving organisational governance and capacity; and
- minimising the burden of regulation.[253]

Most of that agenda has a recognisable relationship to the content of this book. The main exception is the last point on the list, 'minimising the burden of regulation': the argument is that an emphasis on appropriate patterns of governance and judgment by outcomes relieves the necessity for close specification of rules and procedures. (From the perspective of the agencies, this is debatable: one might be forgiven for thinking that a regime based on inspection, close examination and detailed recommendations about activity presented rather more of a burden than a flat statement of rules which requires interpretation and implementation.)

The key questions asked in an inspection are:

1. what the aims of the service are;
2. whether the service meets needs;
3. whether the service delivers value for money;
4. whether the service has been delivering improving value for money;
5. how the service manages performance; and
6. whether the service has the capacity to improve.[254]

Evaluation is primarily, then, a form of policy analysis, but with a stronger emphasis on process than on results. At the same time, the Audit Commission places considerable emphasis on the perspective of users. It writes that:

> We will judge value for money primarily from the perspective of service users. Costs alone do not reflect value. Local context and quality of service are important...[255]

This kind of audit is, recognisably, a form of policy analysis. Unlike most of the policy analyses discussed up to this point, it is strongly informed by external values. The criteria which are being applied go well beyond the question of whether a policy works. They include a commitment to meeting need and priority for the perspective of service users. Other values explicitly referred to in the documentation include commitments to equality, diversity and human rights. The pattern of evaluation is non-partisan, but it suggests a strong political commitment and an important role for the evaluator as a key actor in the policy process.

Evaluation research

Evaluation research is research which is done to assess the value of a programme or activity. There are many specialised texts on this, but we need to avoid the impression, which some of those texts give, that there is a particular technique or set of techniques that is characteristic of evaluation. Evaluation research does what it says on the label. It is an evaluation, and the basis for the evaluation rests in research.

Indicators of effectiveness. A common pattern is to consider indicators of what the activity has done. The available data is usually classifiable in terms of inputs, outputs and outcomes.

- *Inputs* are the activities the service has undertaken – for example, what has been spent, or what has been provided. Examples of inputs are statements like these: '30 places have been provided for people with addiction', 'neighbourhood offices have been placed in every part of the city', or 'there are 73 doctors for every 100,000 people'.
- *Outputs* are the things the service has done. '1,614 homeless people attended our day centre' is an output figure. Every hospital discharge (or 'finished consultant episode') is an output figure.
- *Outcomes* are changes which have happened as a result of the activity. In principle, the outcomes which should be taken into account are those which are clearly and directly attributable to the intervention of the programme; in practice, it is so difficult to identify any direct outcomes that changes in circumstances are often considered enough.

Deciding whether a policy has worked should in theory be based mainly on outcomes rather than inputs or outputs. However, it can be difficult to distinguish between inputs, outputs and outcomes clearly in practice, and it is fairly common for evaluations to slide back and forward between different tests.

Comparing inputs and outcomes: the black box. The idea of the black box is very simple, but it is also counterintuitive – that is, it does not make obvious sense. The idea is drawn from the psychologist, B F Skinner, who argued that the best way to understand people is to look at what goes in and what comes out, and to ignore all the complicated stuff that goes on in people's heads. He suggested we treat the mechanism as a 'black box' – black because it concealed what was going on in the middle (stage magicians use black felt to make things disappear). All you do is to look at what goes in – the inputs – and what comes out – outputs or outcomes. The trick is to ignore everything else you know about a process.

This is easy to do, and it should be straightforward. I find the idea usually causes confusion when I teach the more able postgraduate students, because they find it hard to believe that any technique can be quite so crude and still be useful. An example may help to make it clear. Let us suppose, for example, that we want to establish whether a university is putting lower-class students at a disadvantage in its admissions process. It is possible to imagine the reasons and processes by which this can happen, but we do not need to speculate or hypothesise. What we can do, instead, is to look at what actually happens. We look at the number and range of applicants, we look at their results, and we look to see who is admitted and who is not. We do not need to interview applicants, or people responsible for admissions, or to observe the process, to establish that there is a problem. We would want to do those things once we knew that there was a problem, if we want to work out why and how it is happening; but the first step is to find out whether it is happening or not. That is a simple question, and a simple answer will serve.

Benchmarking. A benchmark is a standard. Often it is expressed as a target or performance indicator. Nominal standards are used to check an agency's performance against an ideal; standards relative to other agencies; or standards within the same agency over time. In some cases, the standard that is applied might not be practically achievable – like the aspiration that every child aged 11 should reach certain educational standards in tests – but the benchmark can still be used to assess both the agency's performance, and the performance relative to others.

The UK government had a flush of enthusiasm for benchmarking in the late 1990s, but this has seemed to fade. There were ambiguities in the idea – for example, as to whether it relies on external standards or self-assessment, how far it can be used comparatively, and what kind of factors could reasonably be benchmarked. Bowerman and Ball argue that the government's expectations for the results of benchmarking were in any case based in a misunderstanding; local authorities in the UK have been using benchmarks since at least the early 1980s, and the idea that endorsing the idea after nearly 20 years' practice would lead to a radical improvement in standards was always illusory.[256]

Benchmarks are more often used to test processes and outputs rather than outcomes. The problem with using them for outcomes (like examination results) is that outcomes can depend on a range of external factors; they can have more influence when the issues are within the control of the agency being benchmarked.

Modelling. One of the weaknesses of simple assessments of outcomes is that it is not always easy to tell what difference the policy might have made. Things may have got better, but can we tell that this has happened because of the policy? Things may not have changed, but might it not have been worse? Evaluations are supposed to test whether something has worked. In principle, if a policy has worked, it has made a difference. There should at least be some added value – something should have happened which would not otherwise have happened. To work out whether that is true, it can help to be able to say what would have happened.

The standard techniques for working out what might have happened were covered in the section on forecasting in Chapter Six. They depend on projections, the modification of parameters and modelling. It should, in principle, be possible to say what would have happened if nothing was done, and in theory it may be possible to say what might have happened with an alternative approach. (These are sometimes referred to as 'counterfactuals'.) It is relatively unusual, however, for evaluations to depend strongly on this kind of calculation, for three reasons. The first reason is that, in most fields, neither the causal models available, nor the core quantitative information available, are good enough to do this sort of work. The Treasury model makes it possible for governments to undertake some of this kind of analysis for national economic policy; there is nothing equivalent for social policy. The second reason is that most social policies, and most local policies, are too small-scale to have much relative impact. There are too many factors. As statisticians put it, there is too much 'noise', and it drowns out any sense of a possible impact. The third reason, which is decisive, is that detailed modelling is not actually necessary. There are ways of deciphering the impact of services without going into details about causes, and without trying to identify all the contributing factors.

Control groups. One common pattern of evaluation research, widely used, for example, in health studies, is to take two or more matched groups and contrast their reactions to different treatments or approaches. The groups are usually matched, although it is possible to cancel out the effect of some differences statistically. A control group is a group to which nothing special is done, to compare the effect of nothing special to the approach which is being evaluated.

This technique is widely used in medical trials, but it is much more difficult to do in ordinary life. The causative factors which are being looked for in medical control trials are generally physical in nature, and control trials are intended to eliminate the influence of extraneous factors. The great problem for medical trials has been the ethical concern that people receiving no treatment are potentially being disadvantaged. That hardly applies in policy settings, where it is fairly common to find that special projects and pilots are tried out in small local settings. Much more of a problem is the issue of 'control'. The kinds of issue that policy research is concerned with are affected by a wide range of problems and issues. The difficultly, then, becomes knowing whether the programme has made a difference, or whether any changes might have happened anyway – or even, when there is no change, knowing whether things would have been better or worse if the programme was not there. The standard approach is to use multivariate statistical analysis, which can determine whether there are any effects after the impact of obvious factors like age, gender, education and income are taken into account. This is subject to some of the reservations made before, about modelling: the information is not that good. But it does make it possible to compare alternative approaches, to control for common social factors, and so to decide that one approach has had more effect than another.

Pawson and Tilley launch a blistering attack on this model of evaluation.[257] Quasi-experimental designs, they argue, have a terrible record of identifying policies that seem to work in one place, but fail to work in others. They believe the flaws in the approach are intrinsic to any quasi-experimental design. Their illustration comes from a high-quality research project comparing the effects of community policing in different locations. The effect of controlling for the environment is to cut out everything that might be said about the 'community' – which, to their mind, also cuts out everything that might offer some insight about how the policy works in practice. 'Our argument', they write, 'is that precisely what needs to be understood is what it is about given communities that will facilitate the effectiveness of a program! And that is precisely what is written out'.[258]

Action research. Action research is primarily used in policy making. Researchers are both examining processes and, at the same time, making decisions about them. The basic model is one of constant experimentation; researchers try out a range of methods, see what works and what does not, and try to select likely approaches. Pioneering examples in Britain have been the CDPs[259] and Educational Priority areas.[260] There are several advantages. One is that researchers are able to try out several approaches. They are able to correct mistakes as they go. By comparison with formal evaluations like randomised control trials, if a policy is not working, researchers are not bound to carry on regardless. The main problem with action research is that the process generates commitment to policy. If a policy is not working, the practitioners and researchers have to be asked why they did not try to do something else instead. Over time, they get locked into a process where they believe that what they are doing is the best thing they can do. No-one wants to feel that they have wasted three years of their life. Both workers and researchers become partisan, and it can be very difficult for them to take a different view.

User perspectives

Service users in the public sector are often members of the public, receiving services on an individual basis – the public, after all, is who the public services are meant to be for. Some social services serve the public directly – social security, social work or the health service. Some, like regeneration services and community development, are aimed at groups or areas, rather than individual recipients. There are many different types of public service, and other public services may equally be serving local businesses (for example, through economic development or city centre management), working with specialist consumers (for example, builders, utility companies, and transport providers) or delivering services to other public sector agencies.

This covers a wide range of activity, but there are three general points which apply. The first is that service users are stakeholders. They have an interest in the policies which are followed, the terms on which services are delivered, and the way that the service performs. I am not proposing here to consider the ethical issues, or the democratic arguments, for user involvement – this chapter is about evaluation, which is a much more limited issue – but there is a growing appreciation that evaluation can be used as a means of empowering users.[261] As stakeholders, users offer an essential counterweight to the views of administrators. The processes of policy analysis tend to have a bias to the administrators; they provide the core information, they are the ones who take policy reform forward, they are the main people with whom policy analysts establish a relationship. But services do not exist for the benefit of the administrators, and their views have to be balanced against the views of other stakeholders.

The second is that users have a particular concern with the delivery of services, and distinct perceptions of the process. I mentioned, when reviewing the formation of aims, Scriven's concern that focusing on the stated aims of a policy can implicitly override the concerns of users.[262] There is a potential danger here, but it does not have to be true; users want services to work, and often their concerns can be expressed in terms of the service's aims. Users' satisfaction or dissatisfaction with the service, their perspective on quality and performance, and their experience of delivery are part of the standard assessments of outcomes.

Users' ability to comment does depend on how directly they are engaged with the service. Sue Balloch and her colleagues suggest that it is difficult to get users to participate in evaluations if the policy being evaluated has not engaged users before the evaluation.[263] This is only half true – users may still appreciate the opportunity to comment, as they did in the case study which follows. Many public services take quantitative surveys of user satisfaction as basic indicators of performance. There are potential problems with these surveys in research terms. People who are asked for views by an agency do not respond neutrally: there is an implicit bias favouring the agency asking the question. In quantitative terms, feedback questionnaires are mainly useful for producing a series of indicators, so agencies know whether they have done better or worse as time goes on. In qualitative terms, they are much more valuable; they give alternative insights and a range of perspectives about what is done, and how else it might be.

The third point, which follows on from the second, is that some users may be able to offer a particular insight into the way that services operate. Complaints from users are a main source of critical incidents, and close examination of complaints makes it possible to identify what has gone wrong, and how to set it right. One local authority (Falkirk Council) explains the benefits as follows:

> A complaints procedure is a positive process that will bring many benefits to the organisation. It will provide the Council with an opportunity to put things right at an early stage, prevent problems escalating into more serious disputes and provide valuable information about weaknesses in our services perceived by our customers. The main benefits of a formal complaints systems include:

- creation of a formal communication channel for service users
- identification of service gaps
- improved service delivery
- benchmarking against defined standards
- information for performance review.

Like the results from feedback questionnaires, complaints and problems can be used to put together indicators (so are positive comments, which are rare in agencies that do not go out of their way to record them). Much more valuable is a detailed, intensive, qualitative examination, which can help to point out issues in the service delivery.

Case study: User perspectives in psychiatric care

This example comes from a qualitative study for a local health board, undertaken with 50 respondents.[264] Patients were given open-ended interviews in depth, on a semi-structured schedule of questions intended to give them the opportunity to identify the issues important to them. For some, those issues related to their personal experience of mental illness; for others, the key issue was the response of the health service. Often this was seen as coercive:

'I got told that if I didn't come here I wasn't getting home…. I took it to mean that they would section me.'

'I lost my freedom being in hospital … I was on medication.'

Two comments, however, were particularly frequent. One was that patients knew very little about their treatment:

'I don't know what's available in the health service…. The only way I can find out I think is by asking the doctor who's very busy and waiting to see the next patient. Nobody has told me how I can find out or where to go. I'm totally confused because I haven't been in this situation before so I don't know.'

The other was that no-one had the time to talk to them. Medical attention was infrequent and harassed staff did not have the time to sit and discuss issues. The main experience of being in hospital was boredom:

'I just sit around and vegetate and things get worse in the hospital.'

Psychiatric patients have often been denied a voice. In former times, this happened because mental illness was treated as a form of incapacity, which invalidated anything they said. This is a misunderstanding of the nature of mental illness. Rogers et al argue:

> Our approach starts from the premise that the views of users of mental health services are valid in their own right. We do not assume that these views are a definitive version of reality or 'the truth', but they are a legitimate version of reality, or a truth, which professionals and policy-makers should no longer evade or dismiss.[265]

Currently, misinterpretations about confidentiality and the ethics of research have become a major obstacle to undertaking work relating to psychatric care. An emphasis on privacy, ethical scrutiny and a presumption against research with vulnerable people has made it difficult for researchers to gain access to psychiatric patients. There is a risk that interviews may be intrusive or distressing, and researchers have to be sensitive to the possibility. But some people see the opportunity as a direct channel of communication to the service:

> 'Just hoping through speaking to yourself and telling you about what happened when I first got to hospital, I just hope that they can put a stop to that....'

This is not a minor reservation to make about dominant ethical standards; if the standards that are being applied stop it happening, there is something wrong with those standards. Giving people a voice is an ethical imperative.

Approaches to evaluation

The literature on evaluation has been characterised by two main approaches. On one hand, there has been a methodology dominated by quantitative, scientific, non-normative analysis. On the other, there is a qualitative, naturalistic, descriptive approach.[266] The World Bank's coverage of evaluation, which is freely available on the internet, is a model of the first type.[267] It has two troubling faults. The first is that for people who are not already schooled in the techniques it is very difficult to understand. I have pointed to several problems with using sophisticated mathematical techniques in social science. Unless users have a very clear understanding of the assumptions behind the models, the character of the relationships being identified, and the ways in which changes in the relationships or in the parameters might affect the results being reported, both the results and any policies based on them are liable to be misconstrued.

The second fault, which is probably more important, is that these techniques rely heavily on the quality of the data that goes into them. The more sophisticated the technique, the more vulnerable it is to inadequate data. The World Bank's advice is aimed at less developed countries – countries which have fewer people involved in formal economic activity, and which tend to be poor. It is almost a tautology to say that they tend to have less developed systems for information gathering and statistical processing. The quality of information needed to make these kinds of technique work is beyond anything in my experience in the UK and Europe, and I am very sceptical about the idea that developing countries are much better equipped to provide the information than developed countries are. Computer programmers refer to the principle of GIGO, which means 'garbage in, garbage out'. Evaluators would do well to bear that in mind.

There is more in this book that supports a qualitative, descriptive approach to evaluation, but there are also reservations about adopting that approach more generally. The focus I have taken on evaluation depends on its position within the structure of a policy analysis. In terms of specific evaluation techniques, the ones that have to be used are the ones that seem most appropriate in context. There is no single model of best practice to follow. Procedures have to be adapted to the problems they are being applied to. There are some issues which require quantitative examination, just as there are some requiring qualitative. But the discussions of consultation and user experiences point to another general issue – not about the style of the evaluation, but the basis on which the evaluation is being carried out. Participative, democratically based evaluations tend to look different from specialised, expert assessments, whether they are quantitative or qualitative.

Policy analysis is also a political activity. If the evaluation is part of a participative process, or it is part of the structure of democratic accountability, the evaluator has to work within the political framework. Political constraints and issues arise even within the narrowly defined position of specialist work for a particular agency. If the evaluator is someone from outside the agency – which is typical of much policy analysis – the evaluation can only have an impact if it is adopted and carried through by someone in the agency. The results are keenly anticipated and felt by staff working on the ground. Part of the task of evaluation is to engage people in consideration, to find people who are likely to take revisions forward. Evaluation calls for discussion, mediation, and responsiveness to people's circumstances. Taylor and Balloch write that evaluation:

> requires the evaluator to master not just quantitative and qualitative research processes but also to develop the political acumen of a skilled negotiator and the sensitivities of an experienced counsellor.[268]

Evaluation is a highly sensitive form of political engagement. It is not a technical exercise.

Exercise

To gain a sense of what evaluations look like in practice, critically examine an audit or Best Value inspection report from www.audit-commission.gov.uk/ or www.audit-scotland.gov.uk/

Policy analysis: developing a checklist

Most of the chapters in this book are concerned with stages in a process, outlined in Chapter Three:

- identifying aims, values and goals:
- assessing the environment;
- identification of methods;
- selection of methods;
- implementation; and
- evaluation.

Although the stages are not really distinct, they can be difficult to separate in practice. They point, however, to a series of issues which almost any policy analysis will have to consider. They can be used as the basis of a checklist.

There are other checklists that people may know. The rational model is one; the Treasury's ROAMEF model (see Chapter Three) is another. Michael Scriven offers a 'key evaluation checklist', with 15 main points:

- context
- descriptions and definitions
- consumers
- resources
- values
- process
- outcomes
- costs
- comparisons
- generalisability (ie, whether there are lessons for others)
- overall significance
- recommendations and explanations
- responsibility and justification
- report and support (ie, follow-up work with agencies), and
- meta-evaluation (that is, evaluation of the evaluation).[269]

These points are all helpful, but the list is difficult to use. The sequence is not very clear, and with a long list of points, it is difficult to know what weight to attach to each element, or how the issues relate to each other. Some of the issues (like generalisability) are less important to policy analysis than they are to other fields. Others which matter for policy analysis, like considering what can go wrong, are hardly considered.

The approach taken in this book is complementary, but different. The sorts of questions that a policy analyst needs to ask are summarised in the table opposite. The questions are not the only questions that can be asked, or that should be, and it may be possible, in some contexts, to leave out some which are inappropriate. This can be used as a checklist, but it does something more important than that – it is also a way of structuring information. The questions reflect a pattern of thought – the kinds of problem that policy analysts need, in practice, to address, and the kinds of issue that they need to consider.

Policy analysis in practice

Key stage	Indicative questions to consider ...	... while reviewing the issues in the light of:
Aims and values	What is the policy supposed to do? What should be done? What should not be done? How will we be able to tell if a policy has achieved its aims?	The policy process Strategic objectives
Assessing the situation	What is happening? What is the evidence? What do stakeholders and key actors have to say? What is likely to happen in the future?	Aims and values
Methods	What are the options? What are the constraints? What resources are there? Are the methods consistent with the aims? What happens if nothing is done? What might go wrong?	Aims and values The assessment of the situation
Effectiveness, efficiency and equity	What are the costs? What are the benefits? Are the methods cost-effective? How can costs be reduced, and benefits increased? Who gains, and who loses?	Aims and values Methods
Implementation	Is the way things are done appropriate to the task? Does the process meet the criteria and standards applicable in this field? How does the process of implementation relate to other work? What is going wrong? What else might go wrong?	Aims and values The assessment of the situation Methods Effectiveness, efficiency and equity
Evaluation	What effects does the policy have? What do those affected think? Has the policy achieved its aims?	Aims and values The assessment of the situation Methods Effectiveness, efficiency and equity The process of implementation

References

Preface

1   W Parsons, 1995, *Public policy*, Aldershot: Edward Elgar;
     J Hudson, S Lowe, 2004, *Understanding the policy process*, Bristol:
     The Policy Press.

Chapter One: The nature of policy analysis

2   M Hill, 2005, *The public policy process*, Harlow: Pearson/Longman.
3   G Smith, 1980, *Social need: policy, practice and research*, London:
     RKP.
4   E Stokey, R Zeckhauser, 1978, *A primer for policy analysis*, New
     York: Norton.
5   A Wildavsky, 1993, *Speaking truth to power*, 4th edition, New
     Brunswick, NJ: Transaction Books, p 16.
6   Wildavsky, 1993, p 16.
7   A Majchrzak, 1984, *Methods for policy research*, London: Sage
     Publications, pp 92-30.
8   R Rhodes, 1999, 'Governance and networks', in G Stoker (ed)
     The new management of British local governance, Basingstoke:
     Macmillan, p xxi.
9   www.aspanet.org/scriptcontent/index_codeofethics.cfm
10   *Policy Evaluation*, 2001, 'Ethical policy analysis', 7(1) pp 15-17.

Chapter Two: The policy process

11   B Hogwood, L Gunn, 1984, *Policy analysis for the real world*,
     Oxford: OUP.
12   D Stone, 1997, *Policy paradox*, New York: Norton.
13   P John, 1998, *Analyzing public policy*, London: Pinter.
14   M Hill, 2005, *The public policy process*, Harlow: Pearson Longman;
     J Hudson, S Lowe, 2004, *Understanding the policy process*, Bristol:
     The Policy Press;
     W Parsons, 1995, *Public policy*, Aldershot: Edward Elgar.
15   See eg P Rossi, H Freeman, 1993, *Evaluation: a systematic approach*,
     London: Sage Publications.
16   J Le Grand, 1997, 'Knights, knaves or pawns?', *Journal of Social
     Policy* 26(2) pp 149-70.

17   R Common, N Flynn, 1992, *Contracting for care*, York: Joseph Rowntree Foundation.

18   G Foster, J Wilson, 1998, 'National Health Service financial management', in J Wilson (ed) *Financial management for the public services*, Buckingham: Open University Press, p 241.

19   M Hill, P Hupe, 2003, 'The multi-layer problem in implementation research', *Public Management Review* 5(4) pp 471-91.

20   R Ashworth, G Boyne, R Walker, 2002, 'Regulatory problems in the public sector', *Policy & Politics* 20(2) pp 195-211.

21   C Handy, 1994, *Understanding voluntary organisations*, Harmondsworth: Penguin, p 134.

22   *The Times*, cited in R Walker, 1986, Aspects of administration, in P Kemp (ed) *The future of housing benefits*, Glasgow: Centre for Housing Research, p 39.

23   R Rhodes, 1999, 'Governance and networks', in G Stoker(ed) *The new management of British local governance*, Basingstoke: Macmillan.

24   C Paton, 1992, *Competition and planning in the NHS*, London: Chapman and Hall;
      B Hudson, 1992, 'Quasi-markets in health and social care in Britain', *Policy & Politics* 20(2) pp 131-42.

25   J Le Grand, 1993, 'Quasi-markets and community care', in N Thomas, N Deakin, J Doling (eds) *Learning from innovation*, Birmingham: Academic Press;
      D Rea, 1998, 'The myth of the market in the organisation of community care', in A Symonds, A Kelly (eds), *The social construction of community care*, Basingstoke: Macmillan.

26   R Forrest, 1993, 'Contracting housing provision', in P Taylor-Gooby, R Lawson (eds) *Markets and managers*, Buckingham: Open University Press.

27   R Hadley, R Clough, 1996, *Care in chaos*, London: Cassell.

28   C N Parkinson, 1958, *Parkinson's Law*, London: John Murray.

29   R Brown, 1986, *Social psychology*, New York: Free Press, ch 13.

30   See G Tullock, 1993, 'The economic theory of bureaucracy', in M Hill (ed) *The policy process: a reader*, Hemel Hempstead: Harvester Wheatsheaf;
      B G Peters, 2001, *The politics of bureaucracy*, London: Routledge.

31   Cited in I Lapsley, 1996, 'Costs budgets and community care', in C Clark, I Lapsley, *Planning and costing community care*, London: Jessica Kingsley Publishers.

32   K Davis, 1966, *Discretionary justice*, Louisiana, LA: Lousiana State University.

33   M Lipsky, 1980, *Street level bureaucracy*, London: Sage Publications.

34   G Smith, 1980, *Social need: policy, practice and research*, London: RKP.

35   M Jackson, B M Valencia, 1979, *Financial aid through social work*, London: RKP.

36   R Singer (ed), 1997, *GP commissioning: an inevitable evolution*, Abingdon: Radcliffe.

37   R Bailey, J Ruddock, 1971, *The grief report*, London: Shelter.

38   R Widdowson, 1976, *Blunt powers – sharp practices*, London: Shelter.

39   www.scotland.gov.uk/Publications/2005/05/23152516/25288

40   P Bridgman, G Davis, 1998, *Australian policy handbook*, Sydney: Allen and Unwin.

Chapter Three: Strategic policy making

41   See eg A Faludi, 1973, *Planning theory*, Oxford: Pergamon;
      N Gilbert, H Specht (eds), 1977, *Planning for social welfare*, Englewood Cliffs, NJ: Prentice-Hall, part 2.

42   HM Treasury, *The green book*, www.hm-treasury.gov.uk/media/785/27/Green_Book_03.pdf, p 3.

43   C Lindblom, 1973, 'The science of muddling through', in A Faludi (ed) *A reader in planning theory*, Oxford: Pergamon.

44   C Lindblom, 1965, *The intelligence of democracy*, New York: Free Press.

45   S Leach, 1982, 'In defence of the rational model', in S Leach, J Stewart, *Approaches in public policy*, London: George Allen and Unwin.

46   C Patton, D Sawicki, 1993, *Basic methods of policy analysis and planning*, Upper Saddle River, NJ: Prentice-Hall, chs 4 and 5.

47   Home Office, 2004, *Developing domestic violence strategies – a guide for partnerships*, London: Home Office Violent Crime Unit, www.crimereduction.gov.uk/domesticviolence46.doc

48   International Monetary Fund, 2003, *Evaluation of poverty reduction strategy papers and the poverty reduction and growth facility*, www.imf.org/external/np/ieo/2002/prsp/013103.PDF

49   D Donnison, 1998, *Policies for a just society*, Basingstoke: Macmillan, pp 133-6.

50   D Donnison, 1998, *Policies for a just society*, Basingstoke: Macmillan.

51   P Marris, M Rein, 1967, *Dilemmas of social reform*, London: Routledge and Kegan Paul.

52   United Nations Fourth World Conference on Women, 1995, *Global platform for action*, New York: United Nations.

53   Cabinet Office, 1999, *Modernising government*, London: The Stationery Office.

54   F MacKay, K Bilton, 2003, *Learning from experience: lessons in mainstreaming equal opportunities*, Edinburgh: Scottish Executive.

55   See eg M Pollack, E Hafner-Breton, 2000, 'Mainstreaming gender in the European Union', *Journal of European Public Policy* 7(3) pp 432-56;
      C Bretherton, 2001, 'Gender mainstreaming and EU enlargement', *Journal of European Public Policy* 8(1) pp 60-81.

56   Eg S Ravazi, C Miller, 1995, *Gender mainstreaming: a study of efforts by the UNDP, the World Bank and the ILO to instituitonalize gender issues*, www.unrisd.org/unrisd/website/document.nsf/ d2a23ad2d50cb2a280256eb300385855/ fc107b64c7577f9280256b67005b6b16/%24FILE/opb4.pdf;
      F MacKay, K Bilton, 2003, *Learning from experience: lessons in mainstreaming equal opportunities*, Edinburgh: Scottish Executive.

Chapter Four: Aims, values and goals

57   Collated by Health Scotland, www.phis.org.uk/pdf.pl?file=pdf/ 35%20Appendix%203.pdf

58   R Titmuss, 1974, *Social policy: an introduction*, London: Allen and Unwin.

59   P Spicker, 1985, 'The legacy of Octavia Hill', *Housing* 21(6) pp 39-40.

60   S Rogers, M Smith, H Sullivan, M Clarke, 2000, *Community planning in Scotland: an evaluation of the pathfinder projects commissioned by CoSLA*, Edinburgh: CoSLA;
      R Stevenson, 2002, *Getting 'under the skin' of community planning*, Edinburgh: Scottish Executive Social Research.

61   J Bryson, 2004, 'What to do when stakeholders matter', *Public Management Review* 6(1) pp 21-53.

62   See eg L Bell, C Stark, 1998, *Measuring competence in physical restraint skills*, Edinburgh: Scottish Office.

63   U Eco, 1987, *Foucault's pendulum*, London: Secker and Warburg.

64   Audit Commission, 2005, *Approach to service inspections*, www.auditcommission.gov.uk/Products/NATIONAL-REPORT/78F62C1A-D68F-4ce0-8276-631A8BAC1B47/ApproachToServiceInspections.pdf, p 8.

65   M Scriven, 1991, *Evaluation thesaurus*, London: Sage Publications, pp 37-8, 178.

66   R Walker, 1994, *Poverty dynamics*, Aldershot: Avebury;
      G Room (ed), 1995, *Beyond the threshold*, Bristol: The Policy Press;
      L Leisering, R Walker, 1998, *The dynamics of modern society*, Bristol: The Policy Press.

67   A Wildavsky, 1993, *Speaking truth to power*, 4th edition, New Brunswick, NJ: Transaction Books, p 29.

68   HM Treasury, *The green book*, www.hm-treasury.gov.uk/media/785/27/Green_Book_03.pdf, p 13.

69   P Ambrose, 2005, 'Urban regneration: who defines the indicators?', in D Taylor, S Balloch (eds) *The politics of evaluation*, Bristol: The Policy Press, pp 48-50.

70   A Etzioni, 1964, *Modern organizations*, Englewood Cliffs, NJ: Prentice Hall, pp 8-10.

71   P Alcock, 2004, 'Targets, indicators and milestones', *Public Management Review* 6(2) pp 211-29.

72   S Boseley, 2003, 'Ambulance queues highlight A&E crisis: targets blamed as patients left waiting hours for handover', *The Guardian*, 16 September, p 7.

73   A Wildavsky, 1993, *Speaking truth to power*, 4th edition, New Brunswick, NJ: Transaction Books, p 29.

74   A Wildavsky, 1993, *Speaking truth to power*, 4th edition, New Brunswick, NJ: Transaction Books, p 30.

75   P Alcock, 2004, 'Targets, indicators and milestones', *Public Management Review*, 6(2) p 221.

76   R Griffiths, 1983, *NHS management inquiry*, London: HMSO.

77   www.performance.doh.gov.uk/nhsperformanceindicators/2002/ha_intro.html

Chapter Five: Assessing the environment I

78   A Majchrzak, 1984, *Methods for policy research*, London: Sage Publications, pp 18-20.

79   B Glaser, A Strauss, 1967, *The discovery of grounded theory*, Harthorne, NY: Aldine de Gruyter.

80   R Pawson, N Tilley, 1997, *Realistic evaluation*, London: Sage Publications, especially ch 3.

81   A Majchrzak, 1984, *Methods for policy research*, London: Sage Publications, p 19.

82   A Sayer, 1981, *Method in social science*, London: Hutchinson.

83   Centre for Public Policy and Management, Grampian Racial Equality Council, 2004, *Community safety for minority ethnic groups in Aberdeenshire*, www.aberdeenshire.gov.uk/ communityplanning/publications/minority.asp

84   C Morrison, 2003, *Ethnic minority business in Fife*, Fife: Fife Council/Fife Racial Awareness and Equality.

85   A Wallace, K Croucher, D Quilgars, S Baldwin, 2004, 'Meeting the challenge: developing systematic reviewing in social policy', *Policy & Politics*, 32(4) pp 455-70.

86   R Freeman, 1984, cited in J Bryson, 2004, 'What to do when stakeholders matter', *Public Management Review* 6(1) pp 21-53.

87   H Catt, M Murphy, 2003, 'What voice for the people? Categorising methods of public consultation', *Australian Journal of Political Science* 38(3) pp 407-21.

88   A Richardson, 1983, *Participation*, London: Routledge and Kegan Paul.

89   D Billis, 1984, *Welfare bureaucracies*, Aldershot: Gower.

90   J Bryson, 2004, 'What to do when stakeholders matter', *Public Management Review* 6(1) pp 21-53.

91   R Elmore, 1978, 'Organizational models of social program implementation', *Public Policy* 26 pp 185-228.

92   P Spicker, J Hanslip, 1994, 'Perceived mismatches between needs and services in the health care of elderly people', *Scottish Medical Journal* 39(6) pp 172-4.

93   See eg F W Murphy, 1977, 'Blocked beds', *British Medical Journal*, 28 May, pp 1395-6;
     J Coid, P Crome, 1986, 'Bed blocking in Bromley', *British Medical Journal*, 10 May, pp 1253-6;
     F Namdaran, C Burnet, S Munroe, 1992, 'Bed blocking in Edinburgh hospitals', *Health Bulletin* 50(3) pp 223-7.

94   J Cohen, 1997, 'Deliberation and democratic legitimacy', in R Goodin, P Pettit (eds), *Contemporary political philosophy*, Oxford: Blackwell.

95   C Brown, 2005, '3600 voice views on parades', *Scotsman*, 23 February.

96   P Spicker, 2005, *Schools in Aberdeen: responses to the 3Rs consultation*, Aberdeen: Aberdeen City Council.

97   B Glaser, A Strauss, 1999, *The discovery of grounded theory*, New York: Aldine de Gruyter.

98   P Spicker, R Martin, 2002, *The future of Scotland's councillors*, Robert Gordon University, www2.rgu.ac.uk/publicpolicy/cppm/councils.pdf

99   R Pawson, N Tilley, 1997, *Realistic evaluation*, London: Sage Publications, ch 6.

100   BBC News, 2003, Census returns of the Jedi, http://news.bbc.co.uk/1/hi/uk/2757067.stm

Chapter 6: Assessing the environment 2

101   J Midgley, D Piachaud, 1984, *Social indicators and social planning, in the fields and methods of social planning*, London: Heinemann, p 39.

102   Cm 5260, 2001, *Opportunity for all*, London: The Stationery Office.

103   H Hoernig, M Seasons, 2004, 'Monitoring of indicators in local and regional planning practice', *Planning, Practice and Research*, 19(1) pp 81-99.

104   Social Disadvantage Research Centre, 2003, *Scottish indices of deprivation*, Oxford: Social Disadvantage Research Centre

105   UNDP (United Nations Development Programme), 1999, *Human development report 1999*, New York: Oxford University Press.

106   OPCS (Office of Population Censuses and Surveys), 1988, *The prevalence of disability among adults in Britain*, London: HMSO; E Grundy, D Ahlburg, M Ali, E Breeze, A Sloggett, *Disability in Great Britain: results of the 1996/97 follow-up to the Family Resources Survey*, www.dwp.gov.uk/asd/asd5/94summ.asp

107   P Spicker, 1993, *Poverty and social security*, London: Routledge, ch 3.

108   OPCS (Office of Population Censuses and Surveys), 1988, *The prevalence of disability among adults in Britain*, London: HMSO.

109   B Jarman, 1983, 'Identification of underprivileged areas', *British Medical Journal* 286 pp 1705-9.

110   Social Disadvantage Research Centre, 2003, *Scottish indices of deprivation 2003*, Oxford: Social Disadvantage Research Centre, p 53.

111   Social Disadvantage Research Centre, 2003, *Scottish indices of deprivation 2003*, Oxford: Social Disadvantage Research Centre, p 53.

112   M Noble, D Firth, C Dibben, M Lloyd, G Smith, G Wright, 2001, 'Meetings on Indices of Deprivation 2000', http://stats.lse.ac.uk/galbrait/indices/OxfordStatement.pdf

113   Cm 5260, 2001, *Opportunity for all*, London: The Stationery Office.

114   DWP (Department for Work and Pensions), 2002, *Measuring child poverty: a consultation document*, London: DWP.

115   J Bradshaw, 1972, 'A taxonomy of social need', in G Maclachlan (ed), *Problems and progress in medical care (7th series)*, Oxford: Oxford University Press.

116   Office of the Deputy Prime Minister, 1999, *Projections of households in England 2021*, www.odpm.gov.uk/embedded_object.asp?id=1156097

117   E Stokey, R Zeckhauser, 1978, *A primer for policy analysis*, New York: Norton, pp 233-6.

118   K Kuntz, M Weinstein, 2001, 'Modelling in economic evaluation', in M Drummond, A McGuire (eds) *Economic evaluation in health care*, Oxford: Oxford University Press.

119   P Spicker, D Gordon, 1997, *Planning for the needs of people with dementia*, Aldershot: Avebury. (The book was based on work funded by the Scottish Office, grant no. K/OPR/2/2/C978).

120   D S Gordon, P Spicker, B Ballinger, B Gillies, N McWilliam, P Seed, W Mutch, 1997, 'Identifying older people with dementia: the effectiveness of a multi-service census', *International Journal of Geriatric Psychiatry* 12(6) pp 636-41.

121   D Kay, 1991, 'The epidemiology of dementia', *Reviews in Clinical Gerontology* 1 pp 55-66.

122   M Scriven, 1991, *Evaluation thesaurus*, 4th edn, p 267.

123   D Wanless, 2002, *Securing our future health*, London: HM Treasury, ch 3, at www.hm-treasury.gov.uk/Consultations_and_Legislation/wanless/consult_wanless_final.cfm

Chapter Seven: Methods, constraints and resources

124   M Scriven, 1991, *Evaluation thesaurus*, 4th edition, p 267.

125   S Walby, 1999, 'The new regulatory state: the social powers of the European Union', *British Journal of Sociology* 50(1) pp 118-40.

126   see eg R Nozick, 1974, *Anarchy, state and utopia*, Oxford: Blackwell.

127 I Berlin, 1969, *Four essays on liberty*, Oxford: Oxford University Press, p xxxix.

128 See eg Cm 6374, *Choosing health*, London: Department of Health.

129 see eg C Murray, 1984, *Losing ground*, New York: Basic Books.

130 A Cawson, 1982, *Corporatism and welfare*, London: Heinemann; M Harrison, 1984, *Corporatism and the welfare state*, Aldershot: Gower.

131 R Nozick, 1974, *Anarchy, state and utopia*, Oxford: Blackwell.

132 F Hayek, 1960, *The constitution of liberty*, London: Routledge and Kegan Paul.

133 M Friedman, R Friedman, 1981, *Free to choose*, Harmondsworth: Penguin.

134 HM Treasury, *The green book*, www.hm-treasury.gov.uk/media/785/27/Green_Book_03.pdf

135 J-J Dupeyroux, 1989, *Droit de la securité sociale*, Paris: Dalloz, p 290.

136 R Lenoir, 1974, *Les exclus*, Paris: Editions de Seuil.

137 C Euzeby, 1991, *Le revenu minimum garanti*, Paris: Editions la Découverte, pp 85-6.

138 F Euvrard, S Paugam, 1991, *Atouts et difficultés des allocataires du Revenu Minimum d'Insertion*, Paris: La Documentation française.

139 E Dugué, D Maillard, 1992, 'Le traitement du chômage au risque de l'individualisation de la formation', in C Guitton, H Sibille (eds) *Former pour insérer*, Paris: Syros.

140 J Bichot, 1992, *Economie de la protection sociale*, Paris: Armand Colin, p 130.

141 P Estèbe, N Haydadi, H Sibille, 1991, 'Le RMI: une raison sociale à la pauvreté?', in *Le RMI à l'épreuve des faits* (collective work), Paris: Syros, p 61.

142 see P Spicker, 1997, 'France', in H Bolderson, D Mabbett, *Delivering social security: a cross-national study*, London: The Stationery Office, pp 124-5

143 P Bachrach, M S Baratz, 1970, *Power and poverty: theory and practice*, Oxford: Oxford University Press.

144 See W Wade, C Forsyth, 2000, *Administrative law*, 8th edition, Oxford: Oxford University Press, part VI.

145 W Wade, C Forsyth, 2000, *Administrative law*, 8th edition, Oxford: Oxford University Press, part VI, pp 242-4.

146 A Jonas, A While, D Gibbs, 2004, 'State modernisation and local strategic selectivity after Local Agenda 21', *Policy & Politics* 32(2) pp 151-68.

147   T Donaghy, 2004, 'Mainstreaming: Northern Ireland's participative-democratic approach', *Policy & Politics* 32(1) pp 49-62.

148   G Stoker, 1999, *The new management of British local governance*, Basingstoke: Macmillan, pp 10-11.

149   P 6, D Leat, K Seltzer, G Stoker, 2002, *Towards holistic governance*, Basingstoke: Hampshire, p 122.

150   D Donnison, 1981, *The politics of poverty*, Oxford: Martin Robertson.

151   P 6, D Leat, K Seltzer, G Stoker, 2002, *Towards holistic governance*, Basingstoke: Hampshire, p 124.

152   M G Sheppard, 1982, *Perceptions of child abuse*, Norwich: University of East Anglia.

153   see eg D Kennedy, 1995, 'Doomsday at the Cabinet Office', *The Times*, 21 August, p 1;
C Doyle, 2005, 'Caring for the survivors', *Daily Telegraph*, 14 January, p 14;
G Bowditch, 1997, Disaster specialist attacks 'monster' of trauma counselling, *The Times*, 29 January, p 6.

154   P Halmos, 1978, *The faith of the counsellors*, London: Constable.

155   R Carkhuff, 1979, *The skills of helping*, Amherst: Human Resource Development Press.

156   See eg V George, P Wilding, 1994, *Welfare and ideology*, Hemel Hempstead: Harvester Wheatsheaf.

157   See D S King, 1987, *The new right*, Basingstoke: Macmillan.

158   R Rushmer, G Pallis, 2003, 'Inter-professional working: the wisdom of integrated working and the disaster of blurred boundaries', *Public Money and Management* 23(1) pp 59-66.

159   Box S, 1987, *Recession, crime and punishment*, London: Macmillan.

160   Social Exclusion Unit, 1999, *Teenage pregnancy*, Cm 4342, London: The Stationery Office.

161   I Allen, S Dowling, 1998, *Teenage mothers: decisions and outcomes*, London: Policy Studies Institute.

162   B Gillam, 1997, *The facts about teenage pregnancies*, London: Cassell.

163   A Giddens, *Sociology*, Cambridge: Polity Press, p 22.

164   See D Pick, 1989, *Faces of degeneration*, Cambridge: Cambridge University Press.

165   See A Deacon, 2002, *Perspectives on welfare*, Buckingham: Open University Press.

166   See eg K Donkor, 2002, 'Structural adjustment and mass poverty in Ghana', in P Townsend, D Gordon (eds) *World poverty*, Bristol: The Policy Press.

167   M Loney, 1983, *Community against government*, London: Heinemann.

168   R Pawson, N Tilley, 1997, *Realistic evaluation*, London: Sage Publications.

169   see eg P Townsend, N Davidson, M Whitehead, 1988, *Inequalities in health*, Harmondsworth: Penguin;
Department of Health, 1998, *Independent inquiry into inequalities in health*, London: The Stationery Office.

170   D Dollar, A Kraay, 2000, *Growth is good for the poor*, www.undp-povertycentre.org/publications/economics/Growth_is_Good_for_Poor-Dollar-Sept02.pdf

171   P Spicker, 2000, *The welfare state: a general theory*, London: Sage Publications.

172   A Sen, 2001, *Development as freedom*, Oxford: Oxford University Press.

173   E Burke, 1790, *Reflections on the revolution in France*, New York: Holt, Rinehart and Winston (1959 edition), p 209.

Chapter Eight: Selecting methods: value for money

174   1999 Local Government Act, cited in J Stewart, 2002, 'Will Best Value survive?', *Public Money and Management* 22(2) pp 4-5.

175   P McMahon, 2005, 'Cost of reaching for the 'Tsars' revealed as £6m', *The Scotsman*, 16 November, p 2.

176   Scottish Public Services Ombudsman, 2005, *Annual report 2004-2005*, www.scottishhombudsman.org.uk/images/downloads/annualreport2005.pdf

177   D Piachaud, J Weddell, 1972, 'The economics of treating varicose veins', *International Journal of Epidemiology* 1(3) pp 287-94.

178   See F Sloan, H Grabowski (eds.), 1997, 'The impact of cost-effectiveness on public and private policies in health care', *Social Science and Medicine* 45(4) pp 505-647.

179   Cited in A Towse, C Pritchard, N Devlin (eds), 2002, *Cost-effectiveness thresholds*, London: King's Fund, p 40.

180   P Gershon, 2004, *Releasing resources to the front line: independent review of public sector efficiency*, London: HM Treasury.

181   P Gershon, 2004, *Releasing resources to the front line: independent review of public sector efficiency*, London: HM Treasury, pp 6-7.

182   D Dawson, R Jacobs, 2003, 'Do we have a redundant set of cost-efficiency targets in the NHS?', Public Money and Management 23(1) p 71.

183   Material obtained on the basis that it would not be identified.

184   Audit Commission, 1993, *Their health: your business*, London: HMSO.

185   HM Treasury, *The green book*, www.hm-treasury.gov.uk/media/785/27/Green_Book_03.pdf, p 26.

186   R Layard, 1972, *Cost-benefit analysis*, Harmondsworth: Penguin Education.

187   D Gould, 1971, 'A groundling's notebook', New Scientist 51, cited in G Mooney, E Russell, R Weir, 1980, *Choices for health care*, London: Macmillan, pp 95-6.

188   H Klarman, 1965, 'Syphilis control programmes', in R Dorfman (ed) *Measuring the benefits of government investments*, New York: Brookings.

189   U Reinhardt, 1997, 'Making economic evaluations respectable', *Social Science and Medicine* 45(4) pp 555-62.

190   J Le Grand, 1982, *The strategy of equality*, London: Allen and Unwin.

191   P Spicker, 2005, 'Targeting, residual welfare and related concepts: modes of operation in public policy', *Public Administration* 83(2) pp 345-65.

192   G Bramley, G Smart, 1993, *Who benefits from local services?*, London: STICERD, London School of Economics and Political Science; G Bramley, 1998, *Where does public spending go?*, London: Department of the Environment.

193   HM Treasury, *The green book*, www.hm-treasury.gov.uk/media/785/27/Green_Book_03.pdf, p 24.

194   Cmnd 9714, 1986, *Paying for local government*, London: HMSO, p 25.

195   Cmnd 9714, p 26.

196   Cmnd 9714, p 124.

197   Cmnd 9714, pp 110-13.

198   Cmnd 9714, p 26.

Chapter Nine: Analysing implementation

199   M Haralambos, M Holborn, 1990, *Sociology: themes and perspectives*, London: Unwin Hyman, p 407.

200   See H Eckstein, 1956, 'Planning: a case study', *Political Studies* 4(1) pp 46-60.

201 M Hill, P Hupe, 2003, 'The multi-layer problem in implementation research', *Public Management Review* 5(4) pp 471-91.

202 J-E Lane, 1993, *The public sector*, London: Sage Publications, ch 4.

203 J-E Lane, 1993, *The public sector*, London: Sage Publications, ch 4.

204 B G Peters, 2001, *The politics of bureaucracy*, 5th edition, London: Routledge.

205 L Blom-Cooper, 1985, *A child in trust: the report of the panel of inquiry into the circumstances surrounding the death of Jasmine Beckford*, London: Brent Council.

206 B Compton, B Galaway, B Cournoyer, 2005, *Social work processes*, Belmont: Brooks/Cole.

207 B Harrington, K McLoughlin, D Riddell, 2001, 'Business process reengineering in the public sector: a case study of the Contributions Agency', in G Johnson, K Scholes (eds) *Exploring public sector strategy*, Harlow: Pearson.

208 C N Parkinson, 1958, *Parkinson's Law*, London: John Murray.

209 H Laming, 2003 *The Victoria Climbié inquiry: report*, Cm 5730, p 67.

210 H Laming, 2003, *The Victoria Climbié inquiry: report*, Cm 5730, p 104.

211 N Flynn, 2002, *Public sector management*, Harlow: Prentice Hall, ch 9.

212 J Newman, S Nutley, 2003, 'Transforming the probation service', *Policy & Politics* 31(4) pp 547-63.

213 P Spicker, 1991, *Access to social housing in Scotland*, Edinburgh: Shelter (Scotland).

214 P Niner, 1975, *Local authority housing policy and practice: a case study approach*, Birmingham: Centre for Urban and Regional Studies.

215 D Clapham, K Kintrea, 1986, 'Rationing, choice and constraint: the allocation of public housing in Glasgow', *Journal of Social Policy* 15(1) pp 51-67.

216 M Calnan, E Ferlie, 2003, 'Analysing process in healthcare', *Policy & Politics* 31(2) pp 185-93.

217 M Calnan, E Ferlie, 2003, 'Analysing process in healthcare', *Policy & Politics* 31(2) pp 185-93.

218 N Parry-Langdon, M Bloor, S Audrey, J Holliday, 2003, 'Process evaluation of health promotion interventions', *Policy & Politics* 31(2) pp 207-16.

219 G Stoker, 1999, *The new management of British local governance*, Basingstoke: Macmillan, pp 10-11.

220 S Carmichael, C V Hamilton, 1967, *Black power: the politics of liberation in America*, New York: Vintage Books, pp 2-6, excerpted at http://smccd.net/accounts/wrightg/race.doc

221 Scarman Report, 1981, p 11, cited in Macpherson Report, 1999, *The Stephen Lawrence inquiry*, Cm 4262-1, London: The Stationery Office, www.archive.official-documents.co.uk/document/cm42/4262/4262.htm, para 6.7.

222 Macpherson Report, 1999, *The Stephen Lawrence inquiry*, Cm 4262-1, London: The Stationery Office, www.archive.official-documents.co.uk/document/cm42/4262/4262.htm, para 6.34.

223 A Sivanandan, 1999, cited in *The Guardian*, 24 February, 'What is individual racism?', www.guardian.co.uk/lawrence/Story/0,2763,208688,00.html#article_continue

224 Macpherson Report, 1999, *The Stephen Lawrence inquiry*, Cm 4262-1, London: The Stationery Office, www.archive.official-documents.co.uk/document/cm42/4262/4262.htm, para 46.28.

225 Macpherson Report, para 6.2.

226 Macpherson Report, para 6.45.

227 See Commission for Racial Equality, 2005, *Good practice*, www.cre.gov.uk/gdpract/index.html

228 See J Elster, 1992, *Local justice*, Cambridge: Cambridge University Press.

229 see eg in Commission for Racial Equality, 2005, *The Police Service in England and Wales*, London: CRE, p 49, www.cre.gov.uk/downloads/PoliceFI_final.pdf

230 Macpherson Report, para 6.45.

231 Commission for Racial Equality, 2005, *Inquiries and formal investigations*, www.cre.gov.uk/publs/cat_fi.html

232 Macpherson Report, paras 6.46-6.48.

233 D Smith, A Whalley, 1975, *Racial minorities and public housing*, London: Political and Economic Planning;
P Spicker, 1988, *Allocations*, London: Institute of Housing;
R Skelington, 1992, *'Race' in Britain today*, Buckingham: Open University Press.

234 F Honigsbaum, 1979, *The division in British medicine*, London: Kogan Page.

235 R Rhodes, 1999, 'Governance and networks', in G Stoker (ed) *The new management of British local governance*, Basingstoke: Macmillan, pp xviii–xxiii.

236 Cited in M Scott, 2003, 'Area-based partnerships and engaging the community sector', *Planning, Practice and Research* 18(4) p 288.

237 DHSS (Department of Health and Social Security), 1974, *Report of the Committee of Inquiry into the care and supervision of Maria Colwell*, London: HMSO.

238 HM Treasury, 2003, *Every child matters*, Cm 5860, London: The Stationery Office, p 5.

239 HM Treasury, 2003, *Every child matters*, Cm 5860, London: The Stationery Office, ch 4.

240 R Griffiths, 1983, *NHS management inquiry*, London: Department of Health and Social Security.

241 A Enthoven, 1985, *Reflections on the management of the National Health Service*, London: Nuffield Provincial Hospitals Trust.

242 J E Powell, 1963, *Medicine and politics*, London: Pitman Medical.

243 J Flanagan, 1954, 'The critical incident technique', *Psychological Bulletin* 51 pp 327-57.

244 *Policy Evaluation*, 2001, 'Ethical policy analysis', 7(1) pp 15-17.

Chapter Ten: The evaluation of policy

245 see eg M Patton, 1997, *Utilization focused evaluation*, London: Sage Publications;
A Clarke, 1999, *Evaluation research*, London: Sage Publications;
P Rossi, H Freeman, 1993, *Evaluation: a systematic approach*, London: Sage Publications.

246 M Scriven, 1991, *Evaluation thesaurus*, London: Sage Publications, pp 178-82.

247 Cabinet Office, 2003, *The magenta book: guidance notes for policy analysis and evaluation*, www.policyhub.gov.uk/ evaluating_policy/magenta_book/chapter1.asp

248 P Bate, G Robert, 2003, 'Where next for policy evaluation?', *Policy & Politics* 31(2) pp 249-62.

249 M Loney, 1983, *Community against government*, London: Heinemann.

250 C Patton, D Sawicki, 1993, *Basic methods of policy making and planning*, Upper Saddle River, NJ: Prentice Hall, p 58.

251 S Cope, J Goodship, 2002, 'The Audit Commission and public services', *Public Money and Management* 22(4) pp 33-40.

252 S Martin, 2004, 'The changing face of public service inspection', *Public Money and Management* 24(1) p 4.

253 Audit Commission, 2005, *Approach to service inspections*, www.auditcommission.gov.uk/Products/NATIONAL-REPORT/78F62C1A-D68F-4ce0-8276-631A8BAC1B47/ApproachToServiceInspections.pdf

254 Audit Commission, 2005, pp 8-12.

255 Audit Commission, 2005, p 24.

256 M Bowerman, A Ball, 2000, 'Great expectations: benchmarking for best value', *Public Money and Management* 20(2) pp 21-6.

257 R Pawson, N Tilley, 1997, *Realistic evaluation*, London: Sage Publications.

258 R Pawson, N Tilley, 1997, *Realistic evaluation*, London: Sage Publications, p 52.

259 R Lees, G Smith, 1975, *Action research in community development*, London: Routledge and Kegan Paul.

260 A Halsey, 1971, *Educational priority*, London: HMSO.

261 I Hall, D Hall, 2004, *Evaluation and social research*, Basingstoke: Palgrave Macmillan, pp 51-2.

262 M Scriven, 1991, *Evaluation thesaurus*, 4th edition, p 37.

263 S Balloch, A Penn, H Charnley, 2005, 'Reflections on an evaluation of partnerships to cope with winter pressures', in D Taylor, S Balloch (eds) *The politics of evaluation*, Bristol: The Policy Press, p 170.

264 P Spicker, I Anderson, R Freeman, R McGilp, 1995, 'User perspectives on psychiatric services: a report of a qualitative survey', *Journal of the Association for Quality in Healthcare* 3(2) pp 66-73.

265 A Rogers, D Pilgrim, R Lacey, 1993, *Experiencing psychiatry: users' views of services*, Basingstoke: Macmillan, p 13.

266 M Patton, 1997, *Utilization-focused evaluation*, Thousand Oaks, CA: Sage, pp 290-9.

267 J Baker, 2000, *Evaluating the impact of development projects on poverty: a handbook for practitioners*, New York: World Bank, available at http://siteresources.worldbank.org/INTISPMA/Resources/handbook.pdf

268 D Taylor, S Balloch (eds) *The politics of evaluation*, Bristol: The Policy Press, pp 251-2.

Policy analysis: developing a checklist

269 M Scriven, 2000, *Key evaluation checklist*, www.wmich.edu/evalctr/checklists/kec.htm

Index

U

ultra vires 105
users of services 7, 56, 58-9, 70-1,
    118, 121, 123, 149-50, 151, 164,
    168. 170, 175-8

V

validity 84-5
value for money 116-7, 129-38, 170
values 49, 54-7, 113
vertical redistribution 140
vision 49, 51-2
voice 56, 78-9, 178

Other titles by Paul Spicker available from The Policy Press

FORTHCOMING

Liberty, equality, fraternity
Paul Spicker, Centre for Public Policy and Management, Robert Gordon University

Paul Spicker's new book takes the three founding principles of the French Revolution – Liberty, Equality, Fraternity – and examines how they relate to social policy today.

The book considers the political and moral dimensions of a wide range of social policies, and offers a different way of thinking about the subject from the way it is usually analysed.

The book is in three main parts, devoted to Liberty, Equality and Fraternity in turn. Each part explores the elements and dimensions of the key concept, its application to policy, its interrelationship with the other two principles, and how policies have developed to promote the principle in society. The conclusion outlines three models of radical politics, based on the main concepts.

Liberty, equality, fraternity is an original, thoughtprovoking book, addressing perennial themes with many topical examples drawn from policy in practice, and offering distinctive insights into socialist and radical thinking.

Hardback £50.00 US$95.00 **ISBN-10** 1 86134 841 X **ISBN-13** 978 1 86134 841 8
234 x 156mm 208 pages tbc September 2006

FORTHCOMING

The idea of poverty
Paul Spicker, Centre for Public Policy and Management, Robert Gordon University

Paperback £15.99 US$28.95 **ISBN-10** 1 86134 888 6 **ISBN-13** 978 1 86134 888 3
Hardbck £55.00 US$85.00 **ISBN-10** 1 86134 889 4 **ISBN-13** 978 1 86134 889 0
240 x 172mm 192 pages tbc January 2007 tbc

Understanding Welfare: Social Issues, Policy and Practice Series

Understanding the finance of welfare
What welfare costs and how to pay for it
Howard Glennerster

"... a brilliant and lively textbook that students will enjoy."
Ian Shaw, School of Sociology and Social Policy, University of Nottingham

Paperback £17.99 (US$26.95) ISBN-10 1 86134 405 8
ISBN-13 978 1 86134 405 2
Hardback £50.00 (US$59.95) ISBN-10 1 86134 406 6
ISBN-13 978 1 86134 406 9
240 x 172mm 256 pages May 2003

Understanding the policy process
Analysing welfare policy and practice
John Hudson and **Stuart Lowe**

"Hudson and Lowe's book provides an excellent review of the issues about the policy process in a changing society and a changing world." **Michael Hill**, Visiting Professor in the Health and Social Policy Research Centre, University of Brighton

Paperback £17.99 (US$28.95) ISBN-10 1 86134 540 2
ISBN-13 978 1 86134 540 0
Hardback £50.00 (US$75.00) ISBN-10 1 86134 539 9
ISBN-13 978 1 86134 539 4
240 x 172mm 304 pages June 2004

Understanding social security
Issues for policy and practice
Jane Millar

"This first-class text provides students with the most up-to-date review and analysis of social security issues. It will fast become the definitive guide to the subject." **Jonathan Bradshaw**, Department of Social Policy and Social Work, University of York

Paperback £17.99 (US$26.95) ISBN-10 1 86134 419 8
ISBN-13 978 1 86134 419 9
Hardback £50.00 (US$59.95) ISBN-10 1 86134 420 1
ISBN-13 978 1 86134 421 2
240 x 172mm 360 pages May 2003

Understanding research for social policy and practice
Themes, methods and approaches
Edited by Saul Becker and Alan Bryman

"Becker and Bryman have successfully combined the virtues of a strong core text with a multi-authored handbook."
Professor Norman Ginsburg, London Metropolitan University

Paperback £19.99 US$32.50 ISBN-10 1 86134 403 1
ISBN-13 978 1 86134 403 8
Hardback £55.00 US$75.00 ISBN 1 86134 404 X
ISBN-13 978 1 86134 404 5
240 x 172mm 448 pages June 2004

To order copies of these publications or any other Policy Press titles please visit **www.policypress.org.uk** or contact:

In the UK and Europe:
Marston Book Services,
PO Box 269, Abingdon,
Oxon, OX14 4YN, UK
Tel: +44 (0)1235 465500
Fax: +44 (0)1235 465556
Email: direct.orders@marston.co.uk

In the USA and Canada:
ISBS, 920 NE 58th Street, Suite 300, Portland,
OR 97213-3786, USA
Tel: +1 800 944 6190
(toll free)
Fax: +1 503 280 8832
Email: info@isbs.com

In Australia and New Zealand:
DA Information Services,
648 Whitehorse Road Mitcham,
Victoria 3132, Australia
Tel: +61 (3) 9210 7777
Fax: +61 (3) 9210 7788
E-mail: service@dadirect.com.au